W9-DIJ-125

DATE DUE

OCT 1 2 1998			
DEC 3 1999			
2 3 2013			

KING PHILIP

The Indian Chief

By ESTHER AVERILL

ILLUSTRATED BY

VERA BELSKY

Linnet Books
Hamden, Connecticut
1993

To Anne Thaxter Eaton

Library of Congress Cataloging-in-Publication Data

Averill, Esther Holden.
King Philip, the Indian chief / by Esther Averill
illustrated by Vera Belsky
    p.   cm.
Originally published: New York : Harper, 1950
Summary: A sympathetic portrait of King Philip, the
Wampanoag sachem who mounted an uprising against the
colonial settlers trying to take his people's land.
1. Philip, Sachem of the Wampanoags, d. 1676—Juvenile literature.
2. Wampanoag Indians—Biography—Juvenile literature.
3. King Philip's War. 1675–1676—Juvenile literature.
[. Philip. Sachem of the Wampanoags. d. 1676.
2. Wampanoag Indians—Biography.
3. Indians of North America—Biography.
4. King Philip's War, 1675–1676.]
I. Belsky, Vera, ill.   II. Title.
E99.W2P483   1993   973.2'4—dc20   92-32156
ISBN 0-208-02357-7 (cloth : alk. paper).
ISBN 0-208-02367-4 (paper : alk. paper).

The paper used in this publication meets the minimum
requirements of American National Standard for
Information Sciences—Permanence of Paper for
Printed Library Materials, ANSI Z39.48-1984.

Printed in the United States of America

CONTENTS

THE NEW ENGLAND COLONIES IN 1675 AND 1676

MASSACHUSETTS COLONY

CONNECTICUT RIVER

BOSTON.

ATLANTIC OCEAN

PLYMOUTH COLONY

PLYMOUTH

HARTFORD

PROVIDENCE.

CONNECTICUT COLONY

RHODE ISLAND COLONY

MOUNT HOPE

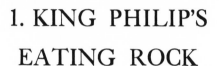

1. KING PHILIP'S EATING ROCK

For a year the Indians, led by their notorious chief, King Philip, had been trying to exterminate the white men in New England, and in the spring of 1676 his painted warriors burned several houses in our village of Plymouth.

Then, suddenly, the tide of war turned in our favor, and in August our Plymouth soldier, Captain Church, caught Philip in a swamp, killed him, and sent his head as a trophy to our village. I glimpsed the trophy as it was carried through the streets to be exhibited on a spike outside of our fort. And on this spike, by order of our government, King Philip's head remained.

At first I was too young to think of King Philip as anything but a devil. Whenever I walked by his head, I tingled with delight in knowing that he was dead and that the war was over and the Indians would never get my scalp.

One day I discovered an elderly colonist gazing at King Philip's skull. "His own father wouldn't recognize him now," observed the gentleman.

"Who was King Philip's father?" I asked.

"Chief Massasoit, who was our friend for forty years."

"Then why did Philip try to kill us?"

"That's hard to answer," said the gentleman. "He was always a mystery."

In the evening, at supper, I asked my parents a question that perplexed me: "Was King Philip really a king?"

"King!" scoffed my mother. "How could any Indian be a king?"

"Why was he called *King* Philip?" I persisted.

My father said, "We colonists often used the title 'king' in our official dealings with the Indian chiefs, and the title stuck to King Philip. Somehow it fitted him."

"It fitted him," my mother said, "because it mocked his pride and arrogance."

"That is only partly true," my father argued. "Many a time I've seen King Philip walking through our streets, dressed in his embroidered deerskin suit and looking like a lord of the wilderness."

"This Philip was no king," my mother interrupted. "He was a fiend who tried to kill us all."

My mother's face assumed that grim look of hers that forbade further discussion of a subject. After that, King Philip's name was rarely mentioned by my parents, and

I seldom heard it mentioned by the parents of the boys I knew. Now that the Indians had been conquered and their land was ours, people seemed eager to forget the horrors of King Philip's rebellion and all that had occurred before it.

From one point of view, nothing more about King Philip needed to be said. Throughout my boyhood his skull remained on exhibit outside of our fort, as a token of his villainy. Yet we children could not help feeling a kind of glorious legend growing up around King Philip.

I felt the legend for the first time when, at the age of nine, I visited some of my young cousins in the neighboring Colony of Rhode Island. My mother had opposed my entering a colony that had been founded by a man like Roger Williams. "A heretic, if there ever was one," she told my father. "He let Baptists, Jews, and even Quakers go there to live."

"The children are the boy's own cousins," my father countered.

I finally went and to my surprise I liked my cousins, though Rhode Island children, because of Roger Williams, were not supposed to be like Plymouth children.

One day my cousins took me to "the rock." They had spoken of this rock and from their voices I had judged it was a prize spot in their wilderness. We walked through pine woods for a mile or so, along an Indian trail, until we reached a clearing near the sparkling waters of the bay. And in the grasses, like a slumbering beast, there lay a huge, gray, flat-topped rock.

"Well, here it is—King Philip's Eating Rock," announced my cousins proudly.

"King Philip?" I protested. "No, this is Narragansett country. King Philip was a Wampanoag and he lived in our colony of Plymouth."

"But sometimes he came here to eat," said Cousin Robert. "Everybody knows that in the first weeks of the war he used to eat here with his wife and son. He had sent them into the Narragansett country to be safe."

"I heard King Philip had a wife and son," I said. "But I know scarcely anything about them."

"His wife was Woolonekamuske," said Cousin Ann, relishing her ability to pronounce so long a name. "Their son—well, I don't know what his name was. I do know he was very young."

"What happened to the wife and son?" I asked.

"The United Colonies sold them into slavery," said Robert. "The boat that carried them off to the West Indies sailed right out there, past Narragansett Bay."

To think of slavery on a bright day such as we had been enjoying sickened me, and to dispel the thought I cried brusquely, "Come, let's play Indian! Let's gather a few berries and have a banquet on King Philip's Eating Rock."

"All right," agreed my cousin Robert. "I shall be King Philip."

"No, let *me* be King Philip," I insisted, rather surprised to find myself wishing to play the part of such a villain. "Why don't you be Philip's ally, Canonchet, the Narragansett chief?"

"Then I shall be the noble warrior, Chief Canonchet," cried Robert, waving his arm as if he held an Indian hatchet.

"And I," said Cousin Ann in a grand manner, "shall be King Philip's wife, Queen Woolonekamuske. And little Bess shall be my son."

We gathered berries, climbed the rock, and feasted. As I look back upon the scene, I realize what an odd-looking group of "Indians" we made: Cousin Ann and little Bess in their long, full-skirted homespun dresses, white neckerchieves and prim white caps, and we boys in somber homespun pants, tight-fitting jackets and broad-brimmed, high-peaked hats. Yet in our imaginations what a feast it was, though all the time I felt that we were sinning and that the Devil might stretch up his hand and carry us away. I believe my cousin Robert sensed my guilty feeling, for he said suddenly:

"Boast not, proud English, of thy birth and blood,
Thy Brother Indian is by birth as good."

"Did you invent that rhyme?" I asked.

"No, Roger Williams did," replied Robert. "I saw it once in a book he wrote about the Indians. Roger Williams was the Indians' friend."

"Yet in the last months of the war," I said, "the Indians burned his house in Providence."

"The war broke Roger Williams' heart," said Cousin Ann. "He grieved because King Philip and Chief Canonchet and all the other good Indians were killed."

"Good Indians?" I queried. "Was King Philip really a good Indian?"

"Of course he was," said Cousin Ann.

"Then why . . . then why . . ." But I did not finish my question aloud. I felt that I must find out for myself whether King Philip was a villain or a hero.

It took me many years to hunt down the truth about King Philip, but as I grew older and my circle of friends widened, I questioned all who had known the Chief before the war. They gave me hints about his character and little anecdotes about some of his kind actions that piqued my curiosity even further.

"This Indian chief was not a villain," I decided. "Then why did he rebel against us? What caused the conflict?"

The Indians themselves could not answer my question because they had been killed, dispersed, or silenced by the war; and as they had never invented an alphabet, they left no written records of their chiefs. But in the government files of Plymouth Colony and our sister colonies, I discovered old treaties, letters, and other documents relating to King Philip. These threw much light on the causes of the conflict and forced me to ask myself the final question: considering the times in which King Philip lived, should he, could he, have acted differently?

2. WHY HE WAS CALLED PHILIP

Philip was born on the Wampanoag hunting grounds in 1637. At first the Indians called him Metacom, or Metacomet, and sometimes Pometacom. He did not receive the English name, Philip, until he was almost a young man. But as he has come down in history as Philip, it is simpler to call him by this name.

Philip's father was Massasoit, chief of the Wampanoag tribe. The Wampanoags were a branch of the great Algonkin family, which included all the brownskinned natives of the New England woods. There are colonists who maintain that "Wampanoag" means "Custodian of the Imperial Shell." Whether or not this is true, the Wampanoags were a proud tribe and in the days of their greatest power had dominated several neighboring tribes that dwelt on the territory stretching westward from the present site of Plymouth village, on the Atlantic coast, to the shores of Narragansett Bay.

A few years before the white men founded Plymouth village, a great plague swept through the wilderness of New England and killed many Indian people. Only four hundred Wampanoag warriors survived the plague, and thus the strength of their tribe was greatly weakened, but its pride remained and was inherited by Philip, the second son of Chief Massasoit.

Philip spent a happy childhood, roaming through the woods and learning how to hunt. The Indians were a race of hunters, and when Philip grew up he might have to pass long winters in the forest to get food for the tribe and deerskins to clothe the people. Young Philip hunted at first with an Indian bow and stone-tipped

arrows and later with a long, heavy rifle such as the English used.

One day Philip asked his father, "Why did the English come here from across the water?"

"Maybe to get firewood," answered Massasoit. "Maybe there was no firewood left for them to burn in their own country."

Neither Chief Massasoit nor any of the early Indians could really understand why the first white men, the English Pilgrims, migrated to New England. The Indians were tolerant of other tribal ways of worshiping the Great Spirit and would have found it difficult to comprehend the religious intolerance which drove the Pilgrims from Old England to seek a corner of the New World where they might worship God as they thought best, without being persecuted.

What Massasoit knew was this: on a bleak day in December (it happened seventeen years before the birth of Philip), a small band of Pilgrims came ashore from a great sailing ship and settled on the rocky coast of Plymouth. The village they founded became the first white settlement in New England, but it would not have lasted if Massasoit had not helped the Pilgrims with his friendship. Before their first hard year was over, he signed a peace treaty with them, and his own people showed them how to plant the Indian corn. Thus the Pilgrims managed to survive.

Years passed, and neither Chief Massasoit nor the men of Plymouth broke the treaty. Each year more white men arrived from England to live in Plymouth Colony, and Massasoit gladly sold them parcels of the Wampanoag hunting grounds. His people had land to spare, and during Philip's boyhood they roamed where they pleased, according to the need to hunt or find new fields in which to plant corn, beans, and squash.

The Wampanoags had no permanent villages, such as the colonists had. An Indian village consisted merely of wigwams that were made by sticking poles in the ground, tying their tops together, and covering the framework with bark, skins, or woven mats. Sometimes a wigwam was pointed and sometimes rounded, but however it was shaped, it could be easily taken down and packed and carried elsewhere.

How different was the white man's cabin, built with square cut logs and a strong roof thatched with grass! Even the smallest cabin had a permanent, determined look. So did the occupants as they cleared the land, plowed the soil, and started their farms. The care these settlers gave their farms amazed the Indians. The only care the Indians gave the land was to burn the brushwood in the forests to make the hunting easier.

Some of the shrewd old Indians, seeing the strength of the white man's ways, grew alarmed. But the white leaders assured the Indians, "There is land enough for us all. The Indians and the English can live side by side in peace, like brothers."

However, as the English grew in strength and numbers and felt surer of their foothold in the New World, their arrogance toward the native race increased and they committed acts that were not always brotherly.

When Philip became old enough to listen to the talk around his father's council fire at night, he could hear the councilors urging the chief to rebel against the colonists before it was too late.

"No," Chief Massasoit would reply. "I have been the friend of the white men ever since they came to live here from across the water. I have a treaty with the men of Plymouth, and I will not break the treaty. Besides, these Englishmen, with their guns and powder, have proved good allies for us against our powerful Indian enemies."

The councilors retorted, "These colonists will soon be stronger than our strongest Indian enemies. Chief, dig up the hatchet now and drive away the colonists before they take our country from us."

"The Plymouth Court will forbid them to take our country," declared Massasoit.

"In the Plymouth Court there can be no justice for the Indians," argued the councilors. "And the Plymouth Court is not the only court that now gives the law to us. There are the courts of Massachusetts and Connecticut."

But Chief Massasoit refused to break his treaty with the colonists of Plymouth. As they expanded their colony, he continued to sell them parcel after parcel of the Wampanoag hunting grounds. The colonists paid him with English hatchets, hoes, and knives, and English coats and cloth. He liked such things.

Gradually most of the Wampanoag hunting grounds passed into English hands. Still Chief Massasoit would not break his treaty of friendship with Plymouth Colony. He could remember the day, some thirty years before, when the Wampanoag crops had withered and his people were hungry. He himself lay in his wigwam, almost at the point of death from hunger. Then one of the first Plymouth governors, Edward Winslow, walked forty miles over the trail to see him and cook a broth for him that helped him to recover.

Chief Massasoit could not forget that act of kindness. He had learned that white men often have shorter memories for such things, but among the Indians the remembrance of a kindly act was handed down from father to son.

In 1656, Chief Massasoit brought his two young sons to Plymouth village and asked the Court to give them English names. He did this partly because English was becoming the principal language of the wilderness, and partly because he wished to show the colonists that he was still friendly toward them and that he hoped his two sons would carry on the friendship after he died.

The sons were tall, strong fellows, wearing deerskin suits embroidered picturesquely with blue and white wampum beads. Their handsome faces had been painted red in the Indian fashion, and their long, straight, coarse black hair had been rubbed with bear's fat until it glistened. But their eyes were their impressive feature.

Through those jet black eyes shone the dignity of the Indian race.

To please old Massasoit, the Court magistrate announced, "The elder son, Wamsutta, shall receive the name of Alexander."

Then, turning to the younger son, a youth of nineteen who was haughtier and more high-strung than his brother, the magistrate declared, "And the younger boy, Metacom, shall receive the name of Philip. Philip and Alexander were the names of two great kings in the ancient history of the Old World."

Yet hardly a colonist in Plymouth believed that any Indian had the right to be a king.

3. HIS MAJESTY
OF MOUNT HOPE

In 1661 old Chief Massasoit died after forty years
of friendship with Plymouth Colony. His tribe mourned
his passing, and his medicine men held ceremonies intended to ease the journey of his spirit to the court of
the southwest god. Of the many gods whose presence the
Indians could feel in the surrounding wilderness, the
greatest was the god of the southwest. The Indians
believed that from his realm came all good things, such
as the warm, benevolent southwest wind, and to his
court, to dwell until the end of time, went the spirits of
good Indians who died.

Massasoit had outlived all the founders of Plymouth
Colony. Bradford, Brewster, Standish, Edward Winslow, and the other great Pilgrims had long been in
their graves, and for many years the old Wampanoag
chief had been the only link with the early days of the
Colony. Now that he, too, had departed, the Plymouth

people could forget that if Massasoit had not helped
their fathers, the Colony would have failed.

To the new, second generation of Plymouth colonists,
the death of Massasoit was, in a sense, a relief, for now
they could bury the past and try their own strength. But
it must be admitted that the strength of many of them,
as far as wisdom, courage, and humanity were con-
cerned, did not equal that of their fathers.

After the death of Massasoit, the elder son, Alexander, became the Wampanoag chief and renewed his
father's treaty of friendship with the Colony. King
Alexander ruled for a year. Then the Plymouth government, disturbed by rumors of his unfriendliness
toward the colonists, sent messengers to him, requesting
him to come to the Plymouth Court for questioning.

The messengers found the new king fishing in the
wilderness with a party of young braves, and he sturdily
refused to cut short his pleasure by hurrying to
Plymouth. So the Plymouth government decided to test
its growing power by dispatching Major Josiah Winslow
with some soldiers to fetch Alexander, and use force if
necessary.

Major Winslow was the son of the early governor,
Edward Winslow, who had been a stanch friend of
Massasoit, but the Major himself, like many of the
second generation of New Englanders, felt little sympathy for the Indians. When Alexander again refused
to go to Plymouth, the Major bade the soldiers seize
him by force. Suddenly, before the Plymouth trip was

over, Alexander died. Did he die of a crushed spirit because he had been seized against his will? Or had the Plymouth people poisoned him? The truth was never known.

The King is dead! Long live the King!

Again the Wampanoags mourned the passing of a leader. But at the same time they rejoiced as tall, twenty-three-year-old Philip became their chief. Not only the Wampanoags, but other tribes throughout New England realized that this was no ordinary princeling stepping into power. Although Philip's ability as a king had not been tested, his personality possessed a curious magnetic power, and Indians from all over the wilderness gathered at his stronghold, the hillock of Mount Hope, to participate in his coronation ceremonies.

Mount Hope stands on the eastern shore of the peninsula called Mount Hope Neck (now called Bristol Peninsula), which juts into the head of Narragansett Bay. The peninsula lies forty miles to the southwest of Plymouth village, and the old Indian trail connecting the two places ran, in Philip's time, through what was mostly somber woodland. But the trail had been well beaten by the feet of Indians and colonists alike, and it formed an artery of communication along which news could travel quickly.

When reports of the great gathering of Indians at Mount Hope reached Plymouth, the government, feeling that there might be trouble brewing, ordered Philip to appear immediately in the Plymouth Court and renew

his father's bond of friendship with the Colony. King Philip interrupted his coronation ceremonies, laid aside his robes of state, took the trail to Plymouth, and renewed the friendly pact. Then he returned to Mount Hope, donned his royal robes once more, and continued the ceremonies.

Philip loved the old Wampanoag ceremonies that had been handed down from generation to generation. He loved fine, colorful costumes, too, for they symbolized the majesty of Indian life. His robes of state consisted of a short tunic belted with a broad band of black and white wampum woven into marvelous patterns of birds, beasts, and flowers. Over the tunic he wore a scarlet blanket, draped like a cloak, and around his head he wound a patterned band of wampum that had a streamer from which two flags fluttered at his back. Around his neck there was a third wampum band from which a bright star was suspended, like a pendant, at his breast. All three bands were edged with red hair that had come from the Mohawk country, west of New England.

After the coronation festivities were over, King Philip settled down to the serious task of ruling a tribe in a world that was constantly growing more difficult for the Indians. He had decided that to the best of his ability he would continue his father's policy of friendship with Plymouth. But the young braves of the tribe were eager to fight the English.

"Chief," they urged, "let us avenge your brother's death. Let us dig up the hatchet now and drive the white men from the country."

"How could we drive them out?" asked Philip. "Our three hundred warriors could not fight all the men of Plymouth and those of her allies, Massachusetts and Connecticut."

"We have allies, too," retorted the braves. "Wetamoo, the squaw sachem of the Pocasset tribe, will give us her three hundred warriors, and Awashonks, the squaw sachem of the Sakonnets, will surely give us her three hundred men."

"Even that would not be enough," said Philip. "We would need all the sachems in the wilderness and all their warriors to fight with us against the English."

The braves were silenced. They knew, as well as Philip, that the Indian tribes inhabiting the New England wilderness had never attempted to unite in the way the English were united. The Indians had always been hunters, and the hunter's way of life had required them to live in fairly small units that could move easily hither and yon in search of game. And because the tribes had never united, they had never been obliged to lay aside their tribal jealousies.

So King Philip tried to defend the rights of his tribe not with the sword but with his diplomatic skill. He studied the ways and the laws of the Englishmen, hoping that with such knowledge he could obtain English justice for his people in his dealings with the Plymouth colonists who continued to push westward and build their settlements closer and closer to Mount Hope.

Philip had the gift of speech. His knowledge of the English language was imperfect, and his letters to the colonists, written through Indian interpreters whose grasp of English was often only a little better than his own, lacked power and effectiveness. But when he pleaded in person, either in his native tongue or in broken English, the colonists could feel the straightness of his thinking and the intensity of his emotions. These qualities, however, did not hold back the white intruder.

By 1670 Plymouth Colony occupied nearly two hundred square miles of land and had crowded the Wampanoags down into Mount Hope Neck, which is only twelve miles long and from one to three miles wide. The tribe had erected their wigwams along the shores of the bay and on the hillock where King Philip dwelt with his wife and little son. Philip had married Woolonekamuske, a Pocasset princess who was the sister of King Alexander's widow, and the son who had been born to them was now four years old. King Philip dearly loved his son and the young queen.

Philip's personal happiness was increased by the affection and esteem of most of his tribe. In fact, if he had thought only of himself, he might have lived contentedly on his green hill, which is certainly one of the fairest spots in New England.

Mount Hope slopes back gently from the shores of the sparkling bay and reaches a height of about two hundred feet. Halfway up the hill, among the groves of pines, rises a whitish cliff in which nature has left a curious depression: a throne of stone upon which King Philip sat when, clad in his scarlet robes of state, he addressed his warriors, as they stood before him in their turkey-feather mantles that fluttered in the breezes.

Unfortunately, the English colonists were moving up to the entrance into Mount Hope Neck. Sometimes their horses and cattle invaded Philip's peninsula and trampled down his cornfields. At the request of the Plymouth government, the settlers erected a fence at the entrance to keep back their livestock. King Philip loathed that fence with all his heart. There had been no fences in the wilderness before the English came.

It is true that the Mount Hope fence kept the English livestock out of King Philip's territory, but he wondered how long it would hold the settlers back. Already they were eying the last remnant of his Wampanoag hunting grounds.

In an effort to preserve Mount Hope Neck for his people, Philip signed a truce with Plymouth in which both parties agreed that he should sell no land to the English during the next seven years. Within a year, however, several of his own Indians were trying illegally to sell a tract to some colonists. All Philip could do was to appeal rather helplessly to Plymouth in the following letter, written through an interpreter:

King Philip desire to let you understand that he could not come to the Court, for Tom, his interpreter, has a pain in his back, that he could not travil so far, and Philip sister is very sik.

Philip would intreat that favor of you, and aney of the majestrats, if aney English or Engians speak about aney land, he preay you to give them no answewer at all. This last summer he maid that promis with you, that he would not sell no land in 7 years time, for that he would have no English trouble him before that time, he has not forgot that you promis him.

He will come as sune as posible he can to speak with you, and so I rest, your verey loveing friend, Philip, dwelling at mount hope nek.

To the much honered
Governer, Mr. Thomas Prince,
dwelling at Plimoth.

Few of the colonists cared whether or not they acquired their land fairly. They had come from the Old World where countries were crowded with people and land was difficult to obtain. Here, in the New World, they were determined to seize what they considered to be their rightful share of a vast wilderness that belonged to no one but the Indians.

The colonists would do almost anything to get land. A favorite method was to intoxicate an Indian. The Indians were poor drinkers, and for this reason the colonists were not supposed to sell them any liquor. But the colonists went on selling it, because a drunken Indian was apt to shoot a horse or a cow or do some other bit of damage for which King Philip, as chief of the Indian's tribe, would have to pay with a slice of land.

By fair means and foul, the colonists continued their

inroads into the Wampanoag country, and some of them managed at last to climb over the Mount Hope fence and settle on Philip's peninsula.

In the past, when the colonists obtained their land unfairly, Philip had tried to get the wrongs righted in the Plymouth Court. But he had learned through bitter experience that the Court was prejudiced against the Indians.

Josiah Winslow, who had followed in his father's footsteps and become the governor of Plymouth, declared publicly, "If at any time the Indians have brought complaints to us, they have received speedy and impartial justice, so that our own people have frequently complained that we erred in showing too much favor to the Indians."

Philip, however, took a different view of the justice handed out by the Plymouth Court. He told some English friends in Rhode Island, "If twenty of our good Indians testify that the English have done them wrong, it counts for nothing. But if one of our worst Indians testifies against me or any other Indian, his word counts, if it pleases the English."

4. KING PHILIP DEFIES THE COLONISTS

In spite of his troubles with the white men, King Philip still visited the settlements. Like his father, Philip had good friends among the English and enjoyed chatting with them under the spreading branches of a great maple or oak. His conversation, however, had taken a serious turn and he openly expressed his dissatisfaction with the policy of Plymouth toward his people.

And then occurred an incident that shocked Plymouth Colony. It was just a trifling incident, but the news spread like wildfire over the trails that led from Mount Hope to the settlements.

"King Philip knocked off the hat of Mr. Cole."

"Hugh Cole of Swansea?"

"Yes, that's the one. He and Philip were supposed to be good friends, but—"

"When did it happen?"

"The other night, at a dance on Mount Hope Neck. The Wampanoags were holding some sort of celebration, and Philip was there, too, and Mr. Cole came up

and rebuked Philip for his rebellious attitude toward our government. And then—"

"Then what?"

"King Philip lifted his heathen brown hand and knocked the hat right off the head of Mr. Cole."

"What insolence! And from an Indian, a savage, a barbarian!"

"He's getting out of control, this Philip of ours."

In the spring of 1671 the Plymouth government sent messengers to Mount Hope, requesting King Philip to appear in the Taunton meetinghouse and renew his father's pledge of friendship with the Colony.

Taunton was a town Philip liked. On the outskirts lay a pond where he often fished, and in the town itself lived his favorite English family, the Leonards. They had come originally from Wales, but, like all English-speaking people in the Colonies, they were called English. The Leonards owned the first iron foundry established in New England, and Philip and his warriors

frequently visited the forge to get their guns repaired. But in spite of his affection for the Leonards, Philip had now passed beyond the point of trusting their colony.

"I will go to Taunton only if the Plymouth government gives my tribe two Englishmen as hostages," declared King Philip. "And while I am in the meetinghouse, the Englishmen must stay on one side of the room. I and my men shall stand on the other."

Plymouth agreed to Philip's conditions and the meeting took place on April 10.

Against one wall of the meetinghouse were lined the white men, looking grim in their dark homespun suits and big slouch hats and breastplates. Each man had a sword at his side and carried a rifle.

Most of the Indians, standing against the opposite wall, carried rifles along with their bows and arrows. But except for the rifles, the Indians, in their odd assortment of deerskins, looked as if they had stepped out of the depths of an ancient wilderness. Their faces were painted with the favorite Indian red and ornamented with patterns of flowers or little crosses or whatever designs pleased the wearer's fancy. And in their jet black hair, worn either long like King Philip's or trimmed down to a scalplock, rose the jaunty feathers of wild birds.

The session with King Philip proceeded slowly. It was conducted through an interpreter, and commissioners from Massachusetts acted as arbitrators between Plymouth and the Indian king. But there was no effort to

iron out the basic difficulties between Philip and Plymouth. Instead, the colonists scolded him as if he were a naughty child. And after he had diplomatically acknowledged his "naughtiness," the Plymouth government forced him to sign a treaty in which he promised, among other things, to surrender all the rifles of his tribe.

In wordiness the treaty resembled many documents to which the Indian chiefs, who could neither read nor write the English language, were often forced to sign their marks. Each chief and councilor had a mark of his own. Sometimes it was an initial, like the "P" which

Philip used. Sometimes it was a symbol, like a bow and an arrow, or a hatchet or an English number, like a seven or an eight.

Here is the Taunton agreement:

Whereas my father, my brother and myself have formerly submitted ourselves and our people unto the King's Majesty of England, and to the colony of New Plymouth, by solemn covenant under our hand; but I, having of late through my indiscretion and the naughtiness of my heart, violated and broken this my covenant with my friends, by taking up arms, with evil

intent against them, and that groundlessly; I being now deeply sensible of my unfaithfulness and folly, do desire at this time solemnly to renew my covenant with my ancient friends, and my father's friends above mentioned, and do desire that this may testify to the world against me if ever I shall again fail in my faithfulness toward them (that I have now and at all times found kind to me) or any other of the English colonies. And as a pledge of my true intentions for the future to be faithful and friendly, I do freely engage to resign up unto the government of New Plymouth all my English arms, to be kept by them for their security so long as they shall see reason. For the true performance of the promises, I have hereunto set my hand, together with the rest of my council.

> In presence of
> *William Davis*
> *William Hudson*
> *Thomas Brattle*
> *The mark* P *of Philip*
> *The mark* V *of Tavoser*
> *The mark* M *of Capt. Wispoke*
> *The mark* T *of Woonchapanchunk*
> *The mark* 8 *of Nimrod*

King Philip and his bodyguard surrendered their guns in Taunton, and he promised to send in the other guns of his tribe when he reached Mount Hope. But the Indians really needed their rifles to hunt with, for the days of the endless forests abounding in game had passed. Plymouth received no more guns from King

Philip, and after a few weeks she wrote to the Massachusetts government and complained of his stubbornness. Plymouth requested advice and assistance from Massachusetts, but added that if assistance were not given, she would send out her soldiers alone to "reduce King Philip to reason."

The wilderness was always filled with Indian eyes and ears, and a letter could not travel to Boston without King Philip's getting wind of it. He arrived in Boston on the same day as the Plymouth letter and went straight to the governor, who read him what Plymouth had written.

King Philip replied to the governor, "The agreements made with Plymouth by my father and renewed by my brother and myself were for friendship and not

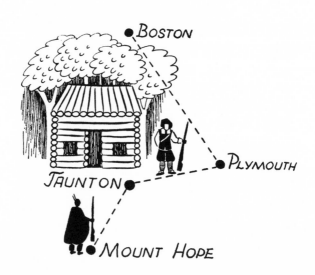

for subjection. I did not know we were the subjects of Plymouth."

King Philip's intelligence and impressive bearing were matched by his eloquent tongue. He spoke well in Boston and for a moment partly won Massachusetts to his point of view. In fact, the Massachusetts governor journeyed down to Plymouth to investigate the matter further and the governor of Connecticut joined him.

At this time there were four colonies in New England and three of them, Connecticut, Massachusetts, and Plymouth, had formed a federation called the United Colonies, for the purpose of mutual aid in dealing with Indian problems. The fourth colony, Rhode Island, had been barred from the federation because of the "heresies," both religious and civil, of her great founder, Roger Williams.

For the benefit of Connecticut and Massachusetts, Plymouth now drew up a list of her grievances against King Philip. They boiled down to this:

1) King Philip had failed to surrender his rifles to Plymouth.

2) He had refused to come to court when summoned.

3) He had entertained Indians from other tribes, some of which were Plymouth's enemies.

4) He had tried to win the favor of Massachusetts by twisting the truth.

5) He had been rude to Mr. Hugh Cole and Mr. James Brown. (This was the same Hugh Cole whose hat had been knocked off by King Philip

at a dance. No one can remember now what
Philip did to Mr. Brown.)

These grievances, the worst that Plymouth could
produce, were too flimsy to justify a war. But Massachusetts and Connecticut, with the white man's solidarity,
stood by Plymouth's side. That autumn the three
United Colonies forced King Philip to appear in Plymouth and sign the following agreement of submission
to Plymouth and the King of England:

1. We, Philip and my council and my subjects, do
acknowledge ourselves subject to his Majesty the King
of England, and the government of New Plymouth,
and to their laws.

2. I am willing and do promise to pay unto the
government of Plymouth one hundred pounds in such
things as I have; but I would intreat the favor that I
might have three years to pay it in, forasmuch as I
cannot do it at present.

3. I do promise to send unto the governor, or
whom he shall appoint, five wolves' heads, if I can
get them; or as many as I can procure, until they come
to five wolves yearly.

4. If any difference fall between the English and
myself and people, then I do promise to repair to
the governor of Plymouth, to rectify the difference
amongst us.

5. I do promise not to make war with any, but with
the governor's approbation of Plymouth.

6. I promise not to dispose of any of the lands that

I have at present, but by the approbation of the governor of Plymouth.

For the true performance of the premises, I the said sachem, Philip of Pokanoket, do hereby bind myself, and such of my council as are present, ourselves, our heirs, our successors, faithfully, and do promise; in witness thereof, we have hereunto subscribed our hands, the day and year above written.

(In the presence of the Court,
  divers magistrates, etc.)
> The mark P of Philip
> The mark † of Wocokon
> The mark [of Uncompaen
> The mark 7 of Samkama

None of the tribute due in pounds and wolves' heads was ever paid by His Majesty of Mount Hope. Plymouth, however, did not press the matter, feeling she had subdued him. She let him go his own way, and he melted into the vast wilderness. For the next three years few colonists worried about the trails he might be following.

Then, to the colonists' alarm, came rumors: "King Philip is sharpening his hatchets. He is getting powder for his rifles. He is plotting war against the English."

Toward the end of 1674, the governor of Massachusetts sent envoys to His Majesty of Mount Hope, asking him to renew his pledge of friendship with the colonists.

But King Philip had changed. His character had

molded, taken shape, and he refused to deal with the colonial delegates. Instead, he drew himself to his full height and with all the royal dignity and pride he could muster, replied, "Your governor is but a subject of King Charles of England. I shall not treat with a subject. I shall only treat with the King, my brother. When he comes, I am ready."

5. A PRAYING INDIAN BETRAYS KING PHILIP

Did Massachusetts inform the King of England that he had an Indian brother, by the name of Philip, waiting for him in the wilderness? It seems unlikely. The English king preferred to let the Colonies handle the Indians without his interference, and there is no evidence that he much cared what happened to the dark-skinned natives of the woods.

Yet there were people in Old England who cared very much what happened to the Indians in New England. These English people believed that the colonists who settled in New England should try to teach the Indians the ways of Christianity and English civilization. Some of the first colonists in Plymouth had believed this, too. Among them was old Governor Edward Winslow, the friend of King Philip's father, Massasoit. Winslow and several Massachusetts colonists had discussed the future of the Indians with the sympathizers overseas.

Out of the discussions there had emerged, in London, a small but earnest group of influential men and women who, for a period of many years, raised money for missionary work among the Indians. The group was called the Society for the Propagation of the Gospel in New England. The Society's most famous missionary was the Massachusetts minister, John Eliot, who is better known as the Apostle to the Indians.

Quietly and tirelessly, the Apostle Eliot, dressed in buckskin, trod the Indian trails that crisscrossed the ancient forests of oak and pine. In the springtime he used to attend the great fishing festivals in which many tribes participated and climbing a high rock, as a minister mounts a pulpit, tell the pagans about the Christians' God.

In this way many Indians became Christian converts, and they were known henceforth as Praying Indians. The Apostle Eliot, however, gathered only a handful of Praying Indians from the Wampanoag tribe. Old King Massasoit clung to the gods of his forefathers and to all the ancient Indian customs. The son, King Philip, did likewise. But Philip was not so easygoing as his father. One day Philip took the gentle Apostle by a button of the coat and shaking the button, declared, "I care no more for Christianity than for the button on this coat."

The Apostle was neither dismayed nor discouraged

by the episode. He disappeared along the trail and made converts elsewhere. This was his life's labor, and as a part of it he translated the entire Bible into the Indian language. His translation was printed, too. It was, in fact, the first Bible in any language to be issued from the printing presses that the colonists, with justifiable pride, had set up in the New England wilderness.

Did the Praying Indians thoroughly understand the Christian doctrine? Probably not. But again, the Apostle Eliot was not dismayed. He was happy if, to begin with, the Indians caught just a little of the Christian spirit. Far better this way, he thought, than for the Indians to continue believing that every stick and stone and waterfall in the wilderness had a pagan god or spirit lurking in it.

The Apostle loved his Indian converts and never tired of laboring for them. But oh, how much there was to do! He had to civilize as well as Christianize them. So he established a few Praying Indian villages for them to live in, and he was helped by his good friend, Major Daniel Gookin, whom the Massachusetts government made ruler of the Praying Indians.

In these villages the Praying Indians were taught to be tidy and clean. Here, for example, was one of the Apostle's rules:

"If any woman shall not have her hair tied up, but hang loose, or be cut as men's hair, she shall pay 5 shillings.

"All men that wear long locks shall pay 5 shillings."

The Apostle also tried to teach the Indians how to farm the land. Having always been hunters, they knew little about farming. The braves considered that farming was work fit only for women. But Eliot wanted the men to work too. So this was another of his rules:

"If any man be idle a week, or at most a fortnight, he shall pay 5 shillings."

Now, King Philip did not wish the English ways to be introduced into the Wampanoag tribe, for he thought they would weaken the strength of his people. Indians should remain Indians, he believed; and his convictions grew as he watched the results of the Apostle Eliot's effort to educate the Indians.

Reading and writing were taught in the Praying Indian villages, and in 1650, in Cambridge, Massachusetts, Harvard College, the first college in New England, opened her doors to Indian students. The charter granted to Harvard in that year stipulated that the college should dedicate herself to "the education of ye English and Indian youth of this country in knowledge and godlyness."

A good brick building, the second building to grace the Harvard campus, was erected for the use of the Indian students. Here they would be lodged and educated free of charge. Their clothing, food, and books would also be supplied to them without cost.

The Apostle Eliot and the other white men who had toiled so hard to bring a college education within reach of the Indians hoped that students from the Praying villages would flock to Harvard in great numbers. Actually, only six young natives enrolled for the first term. Most of these soon grew discouraged and ran back into the wilderness.

Of all the Indians who ever studied at Harvard, only one of them, a lad named Caleb Cheeshateaumuck, stayed long enough to get his bachelor's degree. But during his residence at the college he contracted tuberculosis and though the colonists gave him the best doctoring they could, he died shortly after his graduation.

Few of the Indians who went to Harvard could stand the sudden change in food, housing, and clothing, to say nothing of the strain of studying. Many, like Caleb, became tubercular. The Harvard experiment proved what King Philip had believed all along: the ways of the white men weakened the Indians. Philip made up his mind that his own son should never study books at Harvard.

But the wilderness was changing rapidly. More and more could be heard the babble of English voices and the scratching of quill pens, and eventually King Philip needed a secretary who could read and write English and help him cope with his treaties and correspondence with the colonists. So he took into his employ a Praying Indian named John Sassamon, who had studied for a while at Harvard.

Sassamon, one of the few Wampanoags who had become a Christian, had taught for several years in the Praying Indian villages in Massachusetts. Then a homesickness for the old Indian ways of life got the best of him and he returned to Mount Hope about the time King Philip's troubles with the colonists were reaching a crisis.

As King Philip's private secretary, Sassamon learned much that astounded him, and what he learned threw him into a crisis of his own, during which he had to decide whether he owed his loyalty to the Indians among whom he had been born or to the white men who had Christianized and educated him.

Sassamon made his decision in the autumn of 1674, around the time King Philip told the Massachusetts envoys that he would deal only with the King of England. A few weeks later, Sassamon journeyed to Plymouth village and told the government what he had learned of Philip's secret plans.

"King Philip is plotting to rebel against you," confided Sassamon. "He will go on the warpath and try to drive the white men from New England."

"When will he start to fight us?" asked the government officials.

"Not this spring," replied Sassamon. "King Philip will not be ready in the spring, because he is trying to get all the Indian tribes to join him. But in the following spring, the spring of 1676, King Philip will fight."

Not long after Sassamon had given this information, some Plymouth men found his hat and rifle lying on the ice of a pond fifteen miles from Plymouth village. Near the hat and the rifle was a hole in the ice, and out of the hole the men fished up an Indian's corpse. Its neck was broken and the flesh bruised. The body was identified as that of Sassamon.

6. READY TO DIE
FOR HIS COUNTRY

The colonists believed John Sassamon had been murdered at Philip's request for having betrayed the tribe. Such a penalty would certainly have been demanded by the Indian code of justice. Plymouth, however, saw in this affair an opportunity to take justice into her own hands and give the Indians another taste of her righteousness and strength. She reasoned this way: "Sassamon's body was found within our bounds. All signs indicate that he was murdered. Therefore let the Plymouth Court mete out the punishment the murderers deserve."

The long arm of the Plymouth law reached out into the wilderness, groped around Mount Hope, seized three of Philip's warriors, accused them of murdering Sassamon, and brought them to court for trial.

"It must be a fair trial," said the jurists, putting their heads together and planning how to conduct the proceedings. "By all means, let it be fair, for King Philip and his Wampanoags and all the Indians in New England will be watching us. Let us therefore pick a jury which shall be half English and half Indian."

They picked their Indians almost too carefully. None sat on the jury who were not friendly to the men of Plymouth.

When the trial opened, the three accused Indians pleaded, "Not guilty." Through their interpreter they insisted, "John Sassamon was drowned while fishing. The bruises on his body were made by the ice."

The Court produced its evidence—the only evidence available. This was an Indian who claimed he had seen the trio commit the crime.

The three protested, "That Indian does not speak the truth. He gambled his coat away and when it was returned to him and he was asked to pay for it, he did not wish to pay. So he accused us of the murder. He thought this would please you and make you think he was a better Christian."

The jury deliberated and handed down the verdict, guilty. The three were condemned to death. When they were led to the gallows they still protested that they were innocent, but no one heeded them and two were hanged. As the noose was being slipped around the neck of the third one, he cried, "Those other two really did kill Sassamon. I saw them do it." So the hangman removed the noose and the Indian was reprieved. But the

Court decided to execute him after all and, before the
month was over, he was shot.

The trial had aroused the Wampanoags to a state of
frenzy. They were furious because Plymouth had med-
dled with what they considered a private Indian affair.
The young braves now roamed around the countryside,
shooting English cattle, frightening the wives and children of the colonists, and boasting of the mighty deeds
King Philip would perform.

Soon warriors from other tribes could be seen accom-
panying the Wampanoag braves. In the night, over the
dark Narragansett waters, mysterious canoes with
torches moved toward Mount Hope. High on Mount

Hope a fire would suddenly flare toward the sky and burn for hours. It was King Philip's council fire and the warriors were dancing around it.

On June 14, Governor Josiah Winslow of Plymouth sent two colonists to Mount Hope with a message asking Philip to restrain his own men and send away the visiting braves.

The next day Philip and his councilors conferred with six Rhode Island delegates at Bristol Neck Point, on Mount Hope Neck. The Rhode Island delegates urged Philip to settle his quarrel with Plymouth through arbitration. King Philip replied that he had tried arbitration many times and it had always failed. Arbitration, he claimed, had made him lose most of his tribal hunting grounds. He said that he would rather die than live until he had no country.

Although King Philip expressed his thoughts in broken English, the Rhode Islanders were moved by what he said and repeated it not only to the Plymouth government but also to their friends at home. Rhode Islanders, because they had come under the influence of that great champion of the Indians, Roger Williams, were inclined to feel sympathy for a chief like King Philip. Probably it was a Rhode Island colonist who finally took the trouble to turn King Philip's utterances into the good English they deserved. Here is the final version of the speech in which King Philip, the Wampanoag chief, summed up his grievances against the colonists of New England:

The English who came first to this country were but a handful of people, forlorn, poor, and distressed. My father did all in his power to serve them. Their numbers increased. My father's councilors were alarmed. They urged him to destroy the English before they became strong enough to give law to the Indians and take away their country. My father was also the father to the English. We remained their friend.

Experience shows that his councilors were right. The English disarmed my people. They tried them by their own laws and assessed damages my people could not pay. Sometimes the cattle of the English would come into the cornfields of my people, for they did not make fences like the English. I must then be seized and confined till I sold another tract of my country for damages and costs.

Thus tract after tract is gone. But a small part of the dominion of my ancestors remains. I am determined not to live until I have no country.

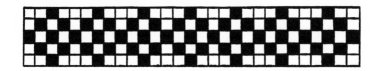

7. THE SETTLER FROM THE BLACK GOOSE COUNTRY

On Wednesday, June 16, an Englishman rode his horse at top speed into Plymouth village. A colonist standing in the narrow street recognized the figure on horseback and called out, "Benjamin Church, do you bring news of the war?"

"Plenty of news," Church called back, but he did not stop. He proceeded straight to the governor's house, swung his long legs to the ground, knocked at the door, and was ushered into the governor's presence.

"Benjamin Church, formerly of Plymouth village and now a settler in our Black Goose country," said Governor Josiah Winslow, as if priding himself on his memory for colony affairs. "Pray be seated, Mr. Church."

The settler from Sakonnet, or the Black Goose country, who was a man in his middle thirties, seated himself
with the air of one accustomed to riding, walking, hunting, plowing, or anything but sitting. His quick, ener-
getic movements contrasted sharply with the slower,
more elegant gestures of Governor Winslow, who was
now the "first gentleman of the Colony."

"Governor Winslow," said Church, "I bring you
news of the war."

"I still hope there will be no war," declared Winslow. "A couple of days ago I sent two colonists to
Mount Hope with a letter for King Philip. In my letter
I requested him to restrain his men and send away the
strangers who have been flocking to Mount Hope. Tell
me, Mr. Church, are things any quieter at Mount
Hope?"

"No," answered Church. "The war dances, which
have been going on for weeks, continue and the braves
have worked themselves to such a pitch that nothing
short of war will satisfy them. They longed to kill your
messengers, Gorton and Brown. Philip managed to prevent it. He told the warriors his father had bidden him
show kindness to Mr. Brown. But Philip can't prevent
the war."

"I know Philip has told the Rhode Islanders that he
is determined not to live until he has no country," observed Winslow. "But that speech of his may have been
just another sample of his famous oratory. Philip can't
really be in any position to fight us. In the first place, he

counted on another year in which to prepare and get his guns and powder. And in the second place, this dream of his to unite all the Indians in New England against us was probably nothing but a pipe dream. Fortunately for us, these barbarians have never been united, nor do they understand the meaning of union."

"Philip's powers of persuasion are very great," argued Church. "He may well have been able to entice the western tribes to his side. But the war will start here in the east, and we can win it here, before it spreads to the west, if we treat our loyal Indian neighbors in the proper way."

"I trust no Indians," retorted Winslow. "Not even those who profess their loyalty to us."

"That is a mistake," objected Church. "We should enlist the loyal braves and use their services in a war that will certainly be fought among the trees and swamps and bushes, in true Indian style. And we could start with my own neighbors, the Sakonnets. I saw Awashonks, the Sakonnet queen, only yesterday when she sent for me to ask my advice. She told me that even though she had old ties with Philip's tribe, she had not made up her mind to join him. After talking with Awashonks and her councilors, I persuaded her to put herself and her tribe under the protection of our government. Then she requested me to speak to you on her behalf. Governor Winslow, what steps shall we take to protect her?"

The governor, skipping over the problem of Queen

Awashonks, said, "I suppose your neighbor on the north, Queen Wetamoo, who rules over the Pocasset tribe, will join Philip. Did you see Wetamoo?"

"I went to see her after I left Awashonks," replied Church. "I found Wetamoo on a hill with just a few of her people. She told me the others had gone to Philip's war dances, against her will.

" 'I fear there will be war,' she said.

"I said, 'Queen Wetamoo, you should go to Rhode Island and seek safety for yourself and the people who have remained with you. And you should send word to the Plymouth governor. You know he is your friend.' "

Governor Winslow smiled wryly. "I daresay this swarthy queen still thinks I poisoned her husband, Alexander."

"Most Indians believe you did," said Church. "But because of their old tribal jealousies, some of the Indians like us none the worse for it. For example, Wetamoo's new husband, Peter Nunnuit, will remain loyal to us. I saw Peter, too. He had just returned from Mount Hope in his canoe."

"What did Peter say?" inquired the governor.

"Peter said the war dances were in full swing at Mount Hope," replied Church. "And he said that Philip had been forced to promise his warriors that they could begin to fight on Sunday, four days from now. But he refused to tell me which towns they would attack first. I myself believe they will attack Swansea, which lies right at the entrance into Mount Hope. Our troops should rendezvous at Swansea."

Governor Winslow ignored the advice. He made Church a captain in the Plymouth army and told him the troops should join the Massachusetts troops at Taunton, eighteen miles northeast of Mount Hope. Taunton lay on the line of march from Massachusetts to Mount Hope, argued Winslow. Then he dismissed the settler from the Black Goose country without indicating in any way how the loyal Indians would be treated.

8. THE FIRST SHOT
OF THE WAR

Swansea, as Benjamin Church had maintained, was the logical place for the Indians to attack first. The little English settlement, consisting of two hundred colonists and forty scattered houses, covered ten acres of land that extended to the very entrance into King Philip's territory on Mount Hope Neck.

Warnings from King Philip himself made it clear that Swansea was in danger. His warnings were carried by Indian messengers to several of his Swansea friends. "King Philip advises you to leave Swansea as soon as you can," said the messengers. "He does not wish to hurt you, but he may not be able to keep his warriors from hurting you when the war breaks out."

Yes, Swansea was in grave danger, yet the inhabitants found it difficult to realize the fact. To them, King Philip was still their neighbor. He had never done them any harm, and some of them had known him rather well. To all of them he had been a familiar figure: tall, proud, and very Indian looking with his coppery skin, long, straight black hair, and flashing black eyes. He had been a picturesque figure, too, often wearing a handsome white serge English coat above his Indian breeches. His elegance was marred by only one thing: a twisted hand. The hand had been permanently twisted when an English pistol accidentally exploded in it.

Sunday, June 20—the day appointed for the outbreak of the war—came round at last, and the peace of Swansea had not yet been disturbed. There was a rumor afloat that the Indians did not wish to fire the first shot because they had adopted an English superstition that the side which fired the opening bullet of a war would be defeated. So far, neither the Indians nor the white men had discharged a gun, and on Sunday morning the colonists of Swansea decided to attend church as usual.

Never had the colonists throughout New England felt such need of God as they had felt in recent months. Terrible omens had been seen and heard at night in many places. Northern lights of scary brilliance had illuminated the sky, troops of ghostly horsemen had been heard clattering through the air, and wolves had howled more hungrily than usual. Many ministers had interpreted these omens as a sign that war was on its way as a punishment to the colonists for their sins. The sins included the wearing of immodest clothes and the failure to attend church regularly.

On the morning of June 20 the colonists of Swansea

were careful to dress modestly for church. The men put on their best black outfits that consisted of broad-brimmed, high-crowned hats, fitted jackets, knee pants, heavy stockings and low-cut, hobnailed shoes. The women dressed themselves in long, full-skirted gowns of sober hue, with a white kerchief at the neck and on the head a white cap or a tidy shawl. As for the children, they donned stiff clothes that closely resembled those of the parents.

One by one the families joined their neighbors on the road to church. Except for the men who carried rifles and the children who kept closer than usual to their mothers, the Sunday procession looked about the same as ever. Only a few colonists, for reasons of their own, remained at home.

Solemnly the procession filed into the wooden church, and slowly the minister opened the service with a

prayer. Then the long, long sermon began. The boys and girls tried their best to keep their minds on the sermon, but occasionally a child's eye would wander to the open window and catch a glimpse of the bright air shimmering between the sky and the fields. And a child's thoughts would dwell for a moment on the Indians who might be lurking in the woods.

Suddenly, in the distance, a rifle cracked. Was it the opening shot of the war? Or was it just the bullet of an Indian hunter killing a deer?

Not another shot was heard, and the service continued. Not until the last amen had been pronounced did the colonists file out of the church and learn that during the service a band of eight young Wampanoag warriors in war paint had loped into the village and going to the door of one of the colonists who had stayed home, asked him, "May we grind our hatchets?"

"This is the Lord's Day," replied the colonist. "Such work cannot be done on the Sabbath. Our God would be displeased."

"We care nothing for your God or for you," declared the Indians. "We will grind our hatchets."

The colonist managed to avoid a quarrel, and the Indians departed.

As they strutted up the road they encountered another Englishman. "Be a good man," they sneered. "Don't tell any lies and don't work on the Lord's Day."

Presently they entered the dwelling of a third colonist and demanded a drink of rum. When he refused to give them any, they threatened him and tried to seize the rum by force. Their rage mounted until at last the colonist, in self-protection, raised his rifle and fired. His bullet hit one of the Indians, who was immediately carried away by his comrades.

Friendly Indians soon appeared in the village and reported that the Wampanoag had not been seriously wounded. They also reported that when the opening shot was fired, King Philip wept. The colonists were surprised at this, because all Indians hated tears.

"Maybe King Philip wept because he has been obliged to fight one year sooner than he planned," thought the colonists. "Yes, maybe he wept because he isn't sufficiently prepared and feels he will lose the war. Probably this war of his will soon come to an end."

9. MOUNT HOPE
IS ABANDONED

Monday, Tuesday, and Wednesday passed without further sign of Philip's Indians. On Thursday the colonists of Swansea fasted and went to the meeting-house to pray. Afterward, as they were walking toward home, a volley from the bushes hit them. Several people were wounded and one man was killed.

While messengers sped toward Plymouth to seek help, the rest of the settlers took refuge in the fortified houses of Swansea. There were four of these garrison houses. One of the best of them, which had a palisade around it, was the home of the Baptist minister, the Reverend John Myles who, a few years before, had brought his little congregation out of Wales and all the way across the ocean so that they might worship God in their own way. The Reverend Mr. Myles, when he left Wales, had never dreamed that someday he would be obliged to guard his Baptist flock against blood-thirsty Indians.

On Monday, June 28, toward evening, the Plymouth and Massachusetts troops that had gathered at Taunton arrived in Swansea and pitched camp next to the Myles garrison. Some had come on horse and some on foot. There were about four hundred soldiers altogether, most of them churchgoing men who had trained in their local militia. But all able-bodied men had been pressed into service, and among the righteous Massachusetts regiments was a godless one composed of sailors and other adventurers gathered from Boston's wharves and prisons. Pirates, waiting to be hanged, had been freed to fight the Indians. These scoundrels had brought hunting dogs to help track Philip to his lair.

All of the soldiers, the righteous as well as the wicked, were eager to capture Philip, and some of the Massachusetts men decided that while twilight lasted they would enter his country and try to find his trail. With the Massachusetts men went tall Captain Church, the settler from the Black Goose country.

As they marched over the bridge that spanned the river near their camp, they were fired on by Indians hidden among the bushes. One Massachusetts man was killed and two were wounded. Most of the soldiers were seized with panic and, abandoning their two wounded comrades, started to flee back to the camp.

But the whiz of bullets did not frighten Captain Church. Coolly and calmly he supervised the removal of the wounded men to safety. As he emerged from his first skirmish with the Indians, he felt in a mysterious

way that King Philip's war was also the war of Benjamin Church.

Next day a band of Philip's painted warriors gathered on the bridge. Tauntingly they yelled to the white troops, "Come and fight us!"

The troops accepted the challenge. They strapped on their bandoliers, from which were hung their powder horns and shot bags, and they seized their rifles. Crack! went the rifles as the troops charged over the bridge. Crack! Crack! Crack! The troops managed to drive the Indians back into the woods. Only one white soldier was seriously wounded in this encounter. The troops felt jubilant as they returned to their camp.

That evening fresh troops arrived from Boston, raising the total number of soldiers to about five hundred.

Next day it rained. But in spite of the rain, the colonial army set forth to catch the rebel, Philip, and his Indians.

Over the bridge went the horsemen with their swords and pistols. Over went the infantry, with their rifles and knives. Over went the pirates with their rifles, knives, and hunting dogs. Over went tall Captain Church, more eager than anyone to capture King Philip. The horsemen were then ordered to spread out and flank the infantry and thus prevent an ambuscade by the Indians. In this formation the colonial troops moved into King Philip's territory on Mount Hope Neck.

The soldiers kept their eyes peeled for Indians. Captain Church who, it was said, could detect an Indian hidden in a bush a mile away, kept his eyes peeled, too. But he saw no more than what his comrades saw. He saw no Indians. The peninsula was utterly deserted and the rain that fell so steadily intensified the desolation of the land.

Here the soldiers discovered the ruins of settlers' houses the Indians had burned. English Bibles, torn to bits by angry Indian hands, lay scattered among the grasses. Farther on, the soldiers came to a cluster of Indian wigwams, still intact, but the occupants had fled. Indian dogs, deserted by their masters, roamed around forlornly.

The troops passed through great Indian cornfields where the bending, green leaves of the plants glistened in the rain. Never a shot was fired. Never an Indian sound was heard.

The troops moved to the east coast of the peninsula and clambered up King Philip's stronghold, the lovely hillock of Mount Hope. They found the long, imposing lodge where Philip and his wife and little son had lived. But there was no trace of any of the royal family.

Some of the soldiers, including Captain Church, climbed to the top of the hill. Because of the rain and the mist, they could not see much of the surrounding country, but Church pointed eastward across Mount Hope Bay.

"If it were a clear day," he told his comrades, "we could see the shore across the bay—the Pocasset shore. The shore is hilly and behind it is a cedar swamp that's seven miles long. I think King Philip and his warriors have gone over to the swamp to hide. We ought to move right over there and catch him now."

But the commanding officers insisted on continuing to hunt for King Philip on Mount Hope Neck. The troops pushed down to the southern tip of the peninsula and back to its entrance, in vain.

Near the entrance they discovered the heads of eight colonists the Indians had killed. The Indians had stuck the heads on poles, this being a custom brought from London by the colonists. Not far from the decapitated heads were some Indian canoes lying abandoned on the north shore of a small river.

Church said, "This proves definitely that King Philip has fled from Mount Hope. I'm convinced he's gone over to the Pocasset country and made the swamp his headquarters. It's a perfect place for him to hide. Besides, he wants to get the Pocasset Indians and my old friends, the Sakonnets, to join him. Now's the time to catch King Philip in Pocasset."

10. KING PHILIP ESCAPES FROM THE POCASSET SWAMP

The officers in command of the colonial army should have followed Captain Church's advice and moved over to the Pocasset swamp in pursuit of King Philip. The army now had five hundred fighting men, while King Philip had scarcely more than his three hundred Wampanoag braves. But the colonial commanders, instead of pursuing and attacking the Indians, remained on the defensive. King Philip's abandoned territory at Mount Hope, with all its ancient Indian associations, cast a spell over the troops, and they began to build a fort there to serve as headquarters.

Some of the men fanned out through the countryside, trampled down King Philip's cornfields, and by destroying the future grain supply of his tribe achieved one kind of victory. But Captain Church would have preferred to win the other kind, the military victory. To achieve this, the troops would have to track down the Indians, and lie in the woods and swamps and fight from behind trees and bushes in the Indian way. Church was delighted when he learned that a regiment of fifty Praying Indians was being sent from Massachusetts to join the army on Mount Hope.

The Indian regiment had been raised by Major Daniel Gookin, the ruler of the Praying Indians of Massachusetts. All the Praying Indians in that colony had sworn allegiance to Massachusetts and were therefore her subjects. When King Philip's war broke out, Major Gookin had asked the Praying Indians to send him one third of their able men. "This was done readily and cheerfully"—to quote Gookin's own words. And from the number, he had chosen fifty of the best warriors.

They arrived at Mount Hope primed for the war-path. Their bodies, naked except for moccasins and breech clouts, were greased to slip right through the hands of the enemy. Their chests were painted with pictures of bears, wolves, and other tribal emblems, and their faces were smeared with gaudy colors to give as fierce a look as possible. For weapons, they carried the usual Indian equipment, bows and arrows, spears, clubs, scalping knives and tomahawks, as well as English rifles.

With their knowledge of wilderness warfare, and their eagerness to fight for Massachusetts, the braves would have made superb allies for the colonists. But it

is a curious and shameful thing to note that the white
soldiers felt superior to their dark brothers-in-arms.
Soldiers like Benjamin Church who had no hatred for
a friendly Indian were few and far between. Most of
the white men felt indignant at having a regiment of
Indians in their midst and called these loyal and valorous
warriors "skulkers behind trees" and all manner of in-
sulting names. False reports of the cowardly behavior
of the Indian allies were soon forwarded to the Massachusetts government by the officers. After twenty-five
days, part of the regiment was sent home. The others
remained with the army for a while longer, but their

service was held in contempt and their advice never heeded.

It is no wonder that the military victories in the first phase of the war in the east fell to King Philip and his braves. His tactics were to strike wherever he could, as swiftly as possible, and gain the upper hand before the slow-moving colonists got their troops into the field.

Philip's braves struck rapid blows at tiny settlements and isolated farms, and at villages like Middleborough and Taunton, though on the eve of the war King Philip had asked his men to spare Taunton if possible. He had asked this because of his friendship with the Leonard family, owners of the Taunton forge where he had often had his rifles mended. But his warriors, now that they were on the warpath, could not always check their frenzy. They did not hurt any of the Leonard family, but they did burn part of Taunton.

No colonist could guess where the Indians would strike next. On a quiet afternoon, or in the middle of the night, or at dawn, a band of naked, yelling Indians would break out of the woods, set fire to a house or a village, shoot men, women, children, and cattle—and vanish. The soldiers dispatched by the colonial commanders to relieve the distressed areas arrived too late, or if they arrived on time were powerless to handle the Indians.

Whether or not King Philip himself took part in any of the early raids is debatable. After a raid the colonists invariably asked each other, "Did you see King Philip? Was he with his warriors?"

And there was always at least one colonist who replied, "Yes, King Philip was there. I saw him. I recognized his tall body and his twisted hand. He led his warriors when they swooped into our town."

But another colonist would protest, "How can any of us be sure? They say King Philip disguises himself when he fights. They say he tries to make himself look like his uncle or goodness knows what. Maybe the Indian you thought looked like King Philip wasn't Philip at all."

"Neighbors," a third colonist would declare, "I'll wager that during this attack on our town, King Philip stood on a ledge of that hill over there and looked down on our flames. He's a new kind of Indian and does the organizing and directing, like an English general, but none of the actual fighting."

It did not really matter whether or not King Philip fought personally in the early raids. His ability as a commander was the thing that counted, and his victories proved that he knew how to plan his campaign and make the most of the fighting resources of his braves. To the utmost advantage he employed the Indians' speed, mobility, and willingness to die in combat.

One day some friendly Indians loped into the army headquarters at Mount Hope. "Wetamoo and Awashonks have joined Philip," they announced.

This was news of the worst sort, for Awashonks, queen of the Sakonnets, had three hundred warriors

under her command. So did Wetamoo, the Pocasset
queen. The news, however, stirred the commanders into
something that might almost be described as action.
They decided to send Captain Church over to the
Pocasset swamp to locate the two queens, whom he knew
personally, and persuade them to withdraw from the
rebellion.

But Church was sent there merely as part of a detach-
ment of thirty-six men commanded by another captain
who knew very little about the swamp. Church and
some of the men got into a skirmish with a band of
Indians at Punkatees (now called Pocasset Neck) and
escaped only by the skin of their teeth. The whole

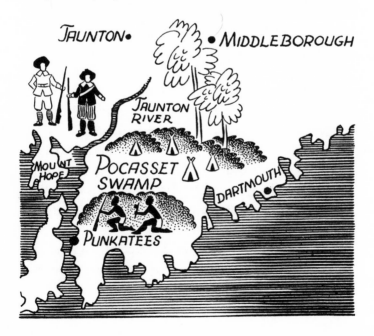

expedition was a failure. Church had not located the queens, and all he had to show for his trouble was a bullet hole in his hat.

The war had been in progress for three weeks before the commanders made up their minds to follow Church's original advice, take a large number of men, and track down King Philip in the Pocasset swamp. Church and the Plymouth men had been sent to relieve the area around Dartmouth, but all the Massachusetts troops were available for the invasion of Pocasset. They set forth on July 18, marched overland for eighteen miles, and reached the swamp late in the afternoon. As they pushed their way into the thicket, the Indians welcomed them with a volley from the bushes, killed five soldiers, wounded many more and then withdrew into the vastness of the swamp.

The encounter took place on the east shore of the Taunton River. Nearby, on a dry upland, stood a group of deserted wigwams, but in one of them the soldiers discovered an old Indian man, sitting alone.

"Where is King Philip?" demanded the soldiers. "Is he hiding in this swamp?"

"Yes," replied the Indian. "King Philip is near. Very near." And he indicated a point of land jutting into the Taunton River.

The soldiers marched toward the point, hopeful that before night came they would capture their prize. But the darkness fell too quickly for them and changed the shapes of things, making the bushes look like Indians and the troops look like bushes, and in this eerie confusion the soldiers began to shoot at each other by mistake. It was time to call a halt.

After a brief conference, the officers decided to withdraw to the edge of the swamp and guard the entrance to the point where King Philip was believed to be hiding. So they ordered a retreat and when they reached the entrance into the point, they were well pleased with their maneuver.

"King Philip is as good as captured," said the officers. "We have trapped him on this point of land that is almost surrounded by the river. Hunger will eventually force him to come out this way. Then we can seize him."

So sure were they of their prize that in the morning they withdrew most of the army and left only a hundred soldiers and a captain to build a fort and wait for King Philip to emerge. The hundred guardsmen and their captain waited. They waited and waited. Day after day went by, and still there was no sign of King Philip.

The soldiers began to wonder, "How long does it take to starve an Indian? Won't Philip ever grow hungry enough to come out of the swamp?"

The fourteenth night of waiting was the last in July. It happened to be an unusually dark night, and the sentinels at the fort kept their ears to the ground. Never a sound of an Indian was heard.

Next morning, however, a band of soldiers scouting far beyond the swamp, near Taunton, sighted King Philip and his warriors fleeing over an open plain toward the Nipmuck country in the west. Some rafts, newly built out of timber from the Pocasset swamp, were found lying abandoned on the bank of the Taunton River. The rafts told more clearly than words the story of King Philip's escape.

A few of the colonial troops pursued King Philip during the rest of the day and all that night. Next day they overtook his warriors, skirmished with them, and then gave up the chase. The Praying Indians who had participated in the pursuit were eager to continue it. They felt that the troops would soon overtake and capture King Philip. But the officers turned a deaf ear to this advice and allowed Philip to escape into the west.

Thus ended the first phase of King Philip's war. His campaign in the east had succeeded and brought death, terror, and destruction to many colonial homes. His departure now eased the tension in the east, as most of his warriors fled with him.

Some of his people who had not been able to escape remained in or around the Pocasset country. Captain Church was sent to parley with them and ask them to surrender. They trusted Church and signed a treaty by which one hundred and sixty of them surrendered to Plymouth Colony. But the ink had scarcely dried on the treaty when the Plymouth government dishonored the terms agreed upon and sold the Indians—men, women, and children alike—into slavery. Some were shipped overseas to Spain and others to the West Indies.

Plymouth's dishonesty and cruel treatment of the

Indians shocked Captain Church. Besides, he was thoroughly disgusted with the way the government and the army had bungled the war in the east. So he retired from the army and moved his family over to the island of Rhode Island. Church, however, was a soldier through and through. Though he was out of the war, he still felt it was his war, and he listened eagerly for news of its developments far away in the west where King Philip had fled.

11. THE SIEGE OF THE BROOKFIELD TAVERN

In the line of King Philip's flight toward the west, all alone in the middle of the wilderness, on the cleared fields near the Quabaug River, stood the tiny English settlement of Brookfield. It consisted of eighteen houses, a tavern, and a meetinghouse. The tavern, being the strongest of the buildings, would serve for the garrison in case of an Indian uprising.

In the spring, King Philip had visited the neighboring Quabaugs, who were a branch of the great Nipmuck tribe, and after his departure, they had grown sullen toward the settlers. But the settlers, confident of their own superiority and power, had refused to believe that the Quabaugs would actually rise up against them.

The Massachusetts government, holding a different view of the situation, had sent a company of cavalry, under the command of Major Simon Willard, to patrol the Nipmuck country, and on July 28, about the time

King Philip was making ready to escape from the Pocasset swamp, a company of twenty horsemen was dispatched from Boston to guard Brookfield.

Captains Hutchinson and Wheeler, who commanded the Boston troops, arranged to hold a peace parley with the Quabaugs on August 2, on a plain three miles from the settlement. With the troops were three Praying Indians who warned the captains against going to the rendezvous. Nevertheless the troops set forth that morning with several Brookfield men and the three Praying Indians. They reached the rendezvous on time, but the Quabaugs were nowhere to be seen.

Hoping to find them farther up the trail, the troops

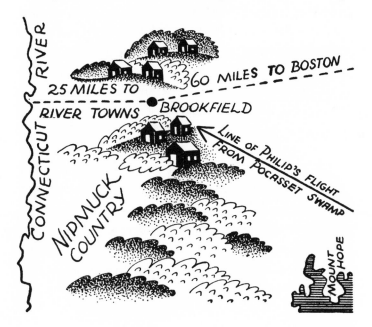

marched along a narrow pass between a bushy swamp and a steep hill. Suddenly from the bushes came a volley. Down went Captain Hutchinson with a fatal wound. Down to their death went eight of the troopers. Down to their death went all the Brookfield men. And out from the bushes leaped the Quabaugs.

One of the Praying Indians was captured, but the other two dashed to Captain Wheeler's side, crying, "Come, Captain, we know the way." And they managed to lead the troops, with all the wounded, up the hill and down a bypath back to Brookfield.

The pitiful condition of the troops when they arrived told the settlers what had happened. From the nearby houses and the surrounding fields, the people rushed to safety in the tavern. They got there just in time. Into the village poured the Quabaugs by the hundreds—two or three hundred of them at least, though it seemed as if all the redskins in the wilderness had descended on Brookfield. With hideous yells the warriors swarmed over to the meetinghouse and adopted it as their headquarters.

Two Englishmen had been sent from the tavern to run to the next town, Marlborough, and ask for help. They had been stopped by the Indians at the end of the street, but had succeeded in returning safely to the tavern. A lad, dispatched from the tavern to his home nearby to get provisions, had encountered a worse fate. The Indians had killed him and cut off his head, and were now kicking the head around like a football, within full view of the tavern.

Soon the Indians, with bloodthirsty war whoops, rushed over to the tavern and began to shoot. The braves were clever at handling the heavy, flintlock rifles that had to be reloaded for each discharge. But the Englishmen inside the tavern remained well hidden at their windows and loopholes and during the day inflicted more damage on the enemy than did the Indians. Not until evening did the Indians kill an Englishman who carelessly poked his head out of an attic window. He was one of the two men who had tried to run to Marlborough for help.

Then the Indians shoved piles of hay against the tavern walls as a step toward burning the wooden structure.

A settler shouted at them through a window, "God is with us and will deliver us from your heathen hands."

"Now see how your God delivers you," cried the Indians, setting fire to the hay.

To their astonishment, as if the white man's God were really watching over His people, some of the settlers emerged from the tavern, quenched the flames and retreated, unharmed, to safety.

Next day the Indians resumed their shooting. During a lull in the attack, the settler who had already tried to reach Marlborough, escaped through the Indian ranks and dashed away at top speed on his mission. The settlers

prayed that Heaven would assist him and that Marlborough would send troops. But if Marlborough did
send troops, how soon would they arrive? Would they
arrive in time to save the people in the tavern?

During the day, the settlers, as they peered through
the tavern loopholes, looked to see if King Philip was
fighting with the Quabaugs. No tall Indian with a
twisted hand was there; but if he had been there, the
settlers would have taken extra pains to shoot the rebel
who had caused them so much misery.

In the evening a band of Indians approached the
tavern with two contraptions made with poles and
barrels set on wheels and piled with hay, flax, and other

combustibles. The inventors proudly pushed their contraptions against the tavern walls, lit the combustibles, and waited gleefully to see the tavern catch fire and smell its occupants being roasted to a crisp. All at once the heavens opened and a mighty rain poured down and soaked the wagons. It was impossible for the braves to start another blaze. They tried and tried, and while they kept on trying, night descended.

An hour later the settlers in the tavern heard the beat of horses' hooves. Who rode the horses? Friends? Or was the rebel, King Philip, leading his Wampanoag warriors into Brookfield? The settlers waited in silence. Then they heard a sturdy English voice giving a command outside in the dark. Captain Wheeler called to his men, "Blow the bugle! Open the doors!"

A soldier blew the bugle, and the horses gathered in the yard beside the tavern. There was a roar of bullets from the Indians, and the thud of men's feet leaping from the horses to the ground. As the tavern doors flew open, in rushed a company of smart dragoons, led by Major Simon Willard, an old man of seventy, but still erect, still handsome, still the first officer of the county.

Willard, while patrolling the region, had heard rumors that Brookfield was on fire. Brushing aside some other Indian business, he had made a forced march through thirty miles of forest to relieve the settlement. His arrival at the tavern was a final blow to the Indians. Many of their plans had gone awry and their patience was exhausted. During the night they shot halfheartedly at the tavern and toward dawn, withdrew. As they passed through the village they set fire to all the houses. Brookfield, except for the tavern and a half-built house, was reduced to ashes.

On this same day, August 5, King Philip, on his westward flight, met the Quabaugs in a swamp twelve miles from Brookfield, and thanked them for having started the war in the Nipmuck country. As a token of appreciation, he distributed three pecks of wampum among three chiefs of the region.

King Philip's visit to the Quabaugs was reported to the Brookfield settlers by the Praying Indian who had fought on the English side, fallen into the enemy's hands, and escaped.

12. WAR ON THE
WESTERN FRONTIER

From Brookfield, King Philip journeyed west to the Massachusetts frontier, twenty-five miles away, in the valley of the Connecticut River. He remained invisible to the settlers who inhabited the valley, but they could feel his presence hovering around them and pressing down on them like a powerful, hidden force from which anything might be expected. To ease their imaginations, the settlers invented many fantastic tales about him.

Among others was a story describing King Philip's arrival among the Nipmucks in the valley. He was said to be wearing a gorgeous wampum mantle, and as he had no money left, he cut up the mantle and distributed the wampum among the great Nipmuck chiefs to buy their services. Actually the services of the Nipmucks did not have to be bought. Here, as elsewhere, the days of friendship with the English had passed, and the chiefs were eager to dig up the hatchet and drive the settlers from the valley.

Meanwhile, troops from Massachusetts and Connecticut patrolled the valley, hoping to prevent the Indians from attacking the river settlements. There were six settlements: Northfield, Deerfield, Hatfield, Hadley, Northampton, and Springfield, ranging in size from Northfield's seventeen families to Springfield's fifty. Hadley, the middle settlement, was chosen as the military headquarters and one hundred and eighty soldiers were dispatched there.

Close to Hadley lived a large number of half-Christianized Indians who had built a fort around their village, claiming that they wished to protect themselves

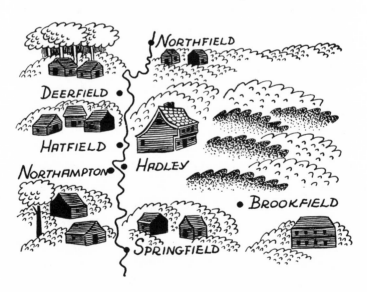

from King Philip's rebels. But the English officers did not trust these Indians and ordered them to surrender their arms.

"No," said the Indians. "We will not give up our rifles now. But we will hand them over to you in a little while."

Instead of keeping their word, the Indians slipped away from their fort on the following night and fled up the river to join King Philip.

Next day the troops from Hadley pursued the Indians, fought them in a swamp near Mount Wequomps (now called Sugarloaf Mountain), and after a fierce skirmish, put them to flight. King Philip is said to have watched the battle from a crag on top of Wequomps, and the crag is today called King Philip's Chair.

On September 1, the Indians attacked Deerfield, and on September 2 they destroyed Northfield. On September 18, they ambushed and killed a regiment of fifty-four young soldiers who were convoying the harvest of corn from the deserted fields of Deerfield to the headquarters at Hadley. The ambuscade took place on the banks of the little stream of Muddy Brook which was afterward renamed Bloody Brook. That summer and autumn the whole green valley of the Connecticut was stained with blood.

On October 5, the Indians attacked Springfield, burned thirty houses and twenty-five barns and killed several settlers and many cattle. It was rumored that

King Philip directed the attack from a lookout near the town, but this may be only one of the many legends that were beginning to be told about him.

True it is that the Indian victories throughout the Connecticut valley in the autumn of 1675 are inseparably linked with the name and the fortunes of King Philip. These were the days of his greatest triumph, and the leaves of the oaks and maples, as they turned to gold and flaming red, seemed to celebrate his ascendancy.

Then the leaves withered and fell from the trees, and only the shapes of the trees—their trunks and forking branches—remained. Stripped of their foliage, the trees and the bushes no longer offered concealment and refuge to the Indians. The trees and the bushes, like the rocks and the river, stood apart in a world of their own that would outlast all the warring peoples in the valley.

Most of the Indians withdrew to their winter quarters, and most of the white troops were ordered to return home. The troops would be needed back in the east to help keep the powerful Narragansett Indians from joining King Philip's rebellion.

13. CHIEF CANONCHET REPLIES

The Narragansetts had been King Philip's neighbors when he lived at Mount Hope, their tribe occupying the western shores of Narragansett Bay, and his the eastern. But the two tribes had been enemies for generations.

On the eve of the war, King Philip had pleaded with Canonchet, the noble Narragansett chief, to bury the hatchet and fight with him against the common foe, the English.

"Let us bury the hatchet," Canonchet had agreed. "Send your wife and son to us for safekeeping. Send your old men and the women and the children of your tribe. My people will shelter them and feed them. But we will not fight with you against the English. Not now. We have no quarrel with Roger Williams and our Rhode Island neighbors."

King Philip had sent his wife and eight-year-old son

and many of the old men and women and children into the Narragansett country. He knew they would be safe there because the Narragansetts were a truly hospitable people.

When the war broke out and the colonists learned that the Narragansetts were sheltering many Wampanoags, the Massachusetts government sent a delegation to Chief Canonchet to question him about his intentions. "I shall fight neither with King Philip nor with the English," the chief replied. "I shall keep peace."

The United Colonies were relieved to learn that Canonchet would remain neutral. He was the greatest warrior in New England and had at least two thousand braves under his command. His tribe was, in fact, the most powerful tribe in New England for it was the only one that had escaped the ravages of the great plague that swept through the wilderness shortly before the white men came. Therefore the Narragansetts had remained strong in numbers.

The Narragansetts had also kept their strength because they had not weakened themselves by adopting English customs. Roger Williams, the first white settler in the Narragansett country, had helped the tribe preserve its ancient Indian ways of living. Though Williams was a minister, he did not try to convert the Indians hastily to Christianity. In this respect he differed from the Apostle Eliot in Massachusetts. Though Williams deplored the paganism of the Indian religion (the branching of one god into many gods), he believed that the Indians in their way could be as religious as the white men. And he asked the colonists to be tolerant of the Indian religion, just as he asked them to respect the religious beliefs of Jews, Quakers, Baptists, and other sects outside the established churches.

But the tolerance which Roger Williams considered necessary if people were to live side by side in peace was not a quality that many colonists possessed. In fact, most of them condemned it, arguing that if a person truly believed that his own ways were right, he would be unable to tolerate the ways of others.

Williams, who had settled first in Massachusetts, was soon banished from that colony because his ideas were looked upon as "too new and dangerous." In midwinter he was obliged to flee through the snowy forests, knowing that none of his own people would dare give him sanctuary. Fortunately in his flight he chanced on the wigwam of King Philip's father, Massasoit, who sheltered him and gave him food and also land to live on. But Plymouth Colony refused to allow such a "heretic" as Mr. Williams to live within her boundaries. In the spring he journeyed into the Narragansett country where Chief Canonicus (the granduncle of Canonchet) received him most hospitably.

"When the hearts of my countrymen and friends and brethren failed me," said Roger Williams in his later years, "the Most High stirred up the barbarous heart of Canonicus to love me as his son to the last gasp."

Canonicus gave Williams land in the Narragansett

country, and the exiled minister remained there and founded Rhode Island Colony, where Quakers, Jews, and other "heretics" took refuge. With Roger Williams as the guiding spirit, the Rhode Islanders and the Narragansetts lived side by side in peace.

The tolerance which Williams practiced was based on understanding. He believed that troubles with the Indians could be avoided if the white men tried to understand the Indian language, customs, and character. With this in mind he wrote a book entitled "Key Into the Language of America," which was published overseas in London as early as 1643.

In the "Key," Williams mentioned many virtues of the Narragansetts. High among these virtues stood their hospitality which he described in the following paragraph:

> Whomsoever cometh in when they are eating, they offer them to eat of that which they have, though but little enough be prepared for themselves. . . . Many a time and at all times in the night, as I have fallen in travel upon their houses, when nothing hath been ready, have themselves and their wives risen to prepare me some refreshing. It is a strange truth that a man shall generally find more free entertainment and refreshing amongst these Barbarians than amongst thousands that call themselves Christians.

Now in July, 1675, the month after the outbreak of King Philip's rebellion, some of the Massachusetts troops that had taken possession of Mount Hope

marched rudely into the Narragansett country, seized
three insignificant old chiefs and forced them to sign an
agreement to deliver all of King Philip's Wampanoags
who could be found within the Narragansett boundaries.
Two coats of trucking cloth would be paid for every
living Wampanoag and one coat for the head of a
Wampanoag. A reward was also offered for the delivery
of King Philip on these terms:

> "Philip Sachem, alive, he or they so delivering,
> shall receive for their pains, forty trucking cloth
> coats; in case they bring his head, they shall have
> twenty like good coats paid them."

But the Narragansetts, clinging to their traditional
code of hospitality, refused to surrender any of the
Wampanoags they were sheltering. As for King Philip,
he was far in the west, fighting in the Connecticut valley.

As the summer drew to a close, it was rumored among
the eastern colonists that King Philip's warriors who
had been wounded in the western battles were being
sent among the Narragansetts to recuperate. Even more
infuriating were the reports that the fires seen along the
Narragansett shores were fires to celebrate the triumphs
of King Philip.

Finally the United Colonies summoned Canonchet
to Boston. On October 18, the commissioners handed
him a treaty which was a renewal of the agreement
signed by the petty chiefs in July. It obliged Canonchet

to deliver to the English within ten days all the Wampanoags, Pocassets, and Sakonnets he was sheltering.

If Canonchet delivered them, they would surely be killed by the English or sold into slavery; of that he was sure. Yet there was little he could do in a hostile town but sign the treaty. After that, the commissioners gave him a handsome English coat trimmed with glittering silver lace and dismissed him. He liked the coat immensely and wore it as he started for home.

When Canonchet reached the Narragansett shores, his old friend, Roger Williams, met him with a canoe to paddle him homeward across the bay.

"Do not break your treaty with the English," warned Williams, who was doing his utmost to keep peace. "Philip is your looking glass. Philip was dead to all advice and is now overset. If you are false to your engagements, we shall pursue you with a winter's war when you shall not, like mosquitoes and rattlesnakes in warm weather, bite us."

How well Roger Williams knew how to use the picturesque phrase that would strike an Indian's imagination! But Canonchet appeared to be unmoved by his friend's warning.

Canonchet said merely, "Philip overset?" in a polite, questioning manner. "I was well treated in Boston," he concluded.

October 28, the last day for the surrender of the

Indian refugees, came round and passed, and not an Indian had been given up. Immediately the United Colonies sent a message of reproof to Canonchet. He answered haughtily, "Not a Wampanoag nor the paring of a Wampanoag's nail shall be surrendered to the English."

14. THE GREAT
SWAMP FIGHT

On November 2, the United Colonies of Plymouth, Massachusetts, and Connecticut decided to raise one thousand extra soldiers and invade the Narragansett country as soon as possible. If the Narragansetts still refused to deliver the refugees, the troops would make war. War, of course, was inevitable.

It was rumored that King Philip himself was staying with the Narragansetts, but the colonists could not be sure. His image was always before their mind's eye. He was the arch-rebel, the demon who must be caught before the war could end. But right now the important business was to fight the Narragansetts. Otherwise, when spring came and the forests burst into leaf, the Narragansetts would surely go on the warpath with Philip.

The United Colonies got ready with all speed. This was the biggest project they had ever undertaken. First, the soldiers had to be outfitted. They had to have good rifles and powder and shot. They had to have warm clothes, because the winter promised to be bitterly cold. They had to have food to carry in their knapsacks— enough food to last them many days.

There were spiritual preparations, too. The war had been so terrible that men's souls were torn asunder, and ministers, still thundering from their pulpits, pointed accusing fingers at the colonists and declared that the war was God's rod of punishment for personal sins. December 2 was set aside as a day of fast and thanksgiving, and the soldiers were warned by the Massachusetts government that "no man shall blaspheme the Trinity on pain of having his tongue bored with a hot iron."

At last the troops were ready. Connecticut had mustered three hundred foot soldiers and one hundred horsemen. Massachusetts and Plymouth together were sending seven hundred foot soldiers and two hundred horsemen. Rhode Island, who, because of her heresies, had never been admitted to the United Colonies, was not allowed to participate officially in the military action. As a matter of fact, most Rhode Islanders were glad to stay out of it, for the Narragansetts had always been their friends.

The troops began marching in the second week in December. Those from Massachusetts and Plymouth, coming down from the north, reached the garrison at Wickford, on the coast of Narragansett Bay, on December 11.

On the military staff of the Plymouth troops was Captain Benjamin Church, who had retired from active service in disgust after the Mount Hope campaign. Even now Church refused to accept a regular command over any of the soldiers. He had his own ideas about the proper way to fight the natives, and as soon as he reached Wickford he called for volunteers and went into the woods to hunt for Indians. The night was clear and the trees and bushes, stripped of their foliage, stood out sharp and bare. There was no danger that a clump of bushes would spring suddenly to life, and Indians, clad in leafy branches from the waist up, would rush forth with hideous warwhoops. Captain Church and his volunteers had good hunting and captured eighteen of the enemy.

But in general, the Narragansett country seemed deserted. For the next few days the troops marched hither and yon and found nothing but a few straggling Indians. One of the stragglers, a fellow named Peter, was taken prisoner and questioned.

"Where are all the Narragansetts?" asked the soldiers.

Peter refused to answer.

"Peter, tell us where the Narragansetts are hiding," the officers commanded. "Tell us, or we'll hang you."

Rather than be hanged, Peter confessed, "Many of them are hiding in the great cedar swamp. I will guide you to them."

On Saturday, November 18, with Peter guiding them,

the troops marched down toward the swamp which lay
nineteen miles southwest of Wickford. Eight miles from
the swamp they joined the Connecticut troops and the
whole army slept that night on the cold, white ground
in the open air. It snowed all night long and when the
men got up at five o'clock next morning their legs were
numb with cold. It was Sunday, too—the Lord's day,
a day of rest. But they got their marching orders just
the same and trudged wearily through the deepening
snow. Peter led the way and at noon they reached the
swamp where Canonchet and his people were hiding.

In ordinary weather the troops would have found
it impossible to enter the swamp. Not only is it a tangle

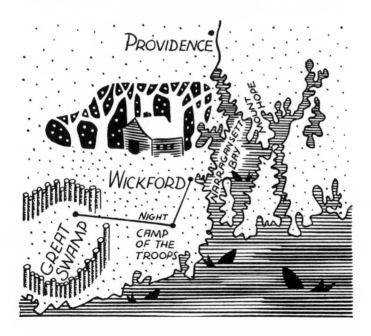

of trees and bushes, but it is wet and treacherous under-
foot. The only dry part is an upland in the middle.

On this upland, according to Peter, Canonchet had
built a fortified village of about six hundred wigwams
and gathered his warriors and many of his people into
it, along with their stores of corn, venison, dried fish,
and nuts. Canonchet had had reason enough to feel
secure on his fortified upland, surrounded by water.
Usually the only approach to it was over logs that served
as footbridges. But the weather had turned so cold that
every inch of water in the swamp was frozen hard.
Never within memory had the swamp been so frozen.
The troops could walk anywhere and approach the
village from every direction.

As they drew near the upland, they could see that
Peter had accurately described its fortifications. A heavy
palisade of upright logs, reinforced with clay and brick
and interspersed with blockhouses, surrounded the village. There was one weak spot: a small, incompleted
section of the palisade, into which the end of a huge
tree trunk had been thrust. The other end of the trunk
lay on the ground outside the palisade in such a way
that the great, sloping log, though guarded by a blockhouse, might serve the soldiers as a footbridge into the
village.

The commanding officers decided to charge up the
log without delay, though the soldiers were exhausted
from the cold and the morning's march and the long

tramp of the day before. As they struggled up the icy, slippery trunk, bullets from the blockhouse whizzed into their midst. Several men were killed, others were wounded, and those on the log were unable to keep their footing. The officers called a retreat.

The soldiers withdrew into the woods, regained their breath, and charged again, under even heavier fire. This time, however, they held their own. Wave after wave of soldiers swarmed over the tree trunk into the fortified village.

Canonchet and his braves were ready for them. There is a legend that King Philip was in the village, fighting

with the rest, but no white man can be sure. As usual, some of the soldiers swore he was there, while others swore he wasn't.

Many of the Narragansett braves fought from their wigwams that had been made bulletproof by shoving stores of corn and other supplies against the inner walls. But the soldiers, fighting like hellhounds, drove the braves into the open and fought them around the wigwams or hand to hand.

The braves had Canonchet to lead them. There was no warrior in all the wilderness as great as he, but the soldiers drove him back. Steady, prolonged fighting in the open was not the Indian way of making battle. Besides, the white men had more rifles than the Indians. Inch by inch Canonchet and his warriors were forced through the village and over the palisade, into the swamp. Some of the old men and women and children escaped, too. But many remained huddled in the wigwams, not knowing what their fate would be.

Darkness was descending and the troops dared not linger for the night. They feared that if they did, Canonchet would rally his braves and counterattack in the morning. Before the troops departed, they set fire to the wigwams. The flames leaped quickly from the fragile walls, and the wind did the rest. The wind, blowing heavily, shot the flames from wigwam to wigwam. Soon all six hundred dwellings were ablaze, and the snowy air was filled with fire and smoke and the shrieks of the trapped Indians and the sickening smell of burned flesh.

Wearily the troops began the march back to Wickford. They left many of their dead near the battlefield, but twenty more they carried to Wickford for burial. Forty wounded men who were unable to walk had to be carried, too. They were borne on crude litters made from boughs and rifles.

The first mile of the march was lighted by the glow from the blazing wigwams. Then the troops plunged along a dark trail through the woods of the swamp. It snowed all the time and the men could barely lift their feet from the heavy blanket on the trail. Icy branches whipped at their faces, and their feet and hands began to freeze. That night twenty-two of the wounded froze to death.

It seemed to the troops that they would never reach Wickford, but they did. At two o'clock in the morning the first of them staggered into the garrison. That same night a vessel sent down from Boston brought them food and other supplies.

But the Narragansetts who had survived were out in the icy woods, having lost many of their people and all the food that should have lasted until spring.

15. HUNGER AND SNOW

The snow did not stop falling. It bowed down the branches of the giant trees and clotted the bushes and muffled the earth. For a month the troops remained snowbound at Wickford, fretting because they could not pursue the Narragansetts and keep Canonchet and the remnant of his band from joining King Philip's rebels in the west.

Toward the middle of January an unexpected thaw sent most of the snow into the earth. While the Connecticut troops marched home to recruit more soldiers, the Massachusetts and Plymouth men set forth on the trail of the Narragansetts. Traces of the Narragansetts were not hard to find. There were footprints in the slushy ground, and the ruins of burned farmhouses, and now and then the skeleton of a horse whose flesh had been eaten by the starving Indians. Above all there were scratches in the earth where the Indians had dug for ground nuts and other edible roots.

The Narragansett tracks led northwest toward the

Nipmuck country, and eventually the troops overtook Canonchet's rear guard in a swamp and killed eighty people. The rest of the braves fled on toward Marlborough and could not be caught. The troops patrolled the country around Marlborough until the end of January. Then hunger and cold forced them to return home.

While the troops were in the field, the Indians had stayed well hidden. No white man had known where they were or what they planned to do. Then, on January 24, a Praying Indian brought news of them to Major Daniel Gookin, the ruler of the Praying Indians of Massachusetts.

Like his friend, the Apostle Eliot, Major Gookin had

devoted most of his life to serving the Indians who wished to live like Christians. And like the Apostle, he had labored all during the war to protect them. For doing this, he had been threatened and insulted by the colonists in the streets of Boston.

At the beginning of the war, most of the Praying Indians had tried to serve their adopted country as best they could. They had offered to fight for her and to build a fort around each of their villages. As their fourteen villages almost encircled Massachusetts, the offer, if it had been accepted, would have shortened the war. But Massachusetts rejected the help of the Praying Indians because she coveted the land on which they lived.

In August, 1675, the government ordered the Praying Indians to move from their villages to special reservations. No longer were they free to hunt, look after their cattle, and tend their cornfields. The majority of able-bodied men, in disgust, soon joined King Philip's rebels. In the winter of 1675-1676 only about five hundred Christian Indians—most of them old men, women, and children—were still loyal to Massachusetts. These were forced to live in isolation on little Deer Island, in Boston Bay, where they suffered greatly from hunger and confinement.

On December 28, nine days after the great swamp fight in the Narragansett country, two of the best men on Deer Island were picked by the Apostle Eliot to journey into the wilderness and spy on the rebels.

The spy who returned on January 24 told Major Gookin, "The rebel tribes are living in several places in the Nipmuck country. When the trees begin to leaf, the tribes will get together and fight. They will fight hard and burn many towns."

"Where is King Philip?" asked Major Gookin.

"King Philip is beyond the Connecticut River, near Fort Albany," said the spy. "He is trying to get the Mohawks to join his rebellion."

"Are the rebels well supplied with guns and powder?" asked the major.

"They have enough for now," replied the Indian. "And they boast that the French in Canada will give them some more, because the French would like to see the English driven out of New England."

"How are the Indians managing for food?" inquired the major.

"They eat venison and corn," said the Indian. "They get corn from the deserted settlements. They eat ground nuts, too."

But venison and corn were not as plentiful as the spy had thought. Starvation stalked among the homeless tribes. Winter had never been a fighting time for Indians because the snow betrayed their steps and the bare woods refused to give shelter. This winter, however, the rebels must fight and raid the English settlements for food— or die of hunger. So at the end of January, when the troops departed from the Nipmuck country, the rebels fought.

They fought with guns and they fought with fire. The great swamp fight had taught them what a mighty weapon fire can be, and with torches and flaming arrows they fired farmhouses and settlements throughout the Nipmuck country.

On February 10, a band of warriors swooped into the town of Lancaster, killed many cattle and several colonists, and carried more than a score of people into captivity.

On February 21, the Indians attacked Medfield, seventeen miles from Boston, and fought with the soldiers who had been sent to guard the settlement. During the battle some of the soldiers saw—or believed they saw—King Philip leaping the fences on a great black horse and urging the braves to do their best. But this image of him was merely a trick of overexcited imaginations. King Philip was still in the west, trying to get the Mohawks to join his rebellion.

It is therefore improbable that King Philip had anything to do personally with the following note that was found on a bridge when the soldiers drove the Indians back from Medfield. The note had been stuck in a cleft of a post and ran as follows:

Know by this paper that the Indians that thou has provoked to wrath and anger will war this twenty-one years, if you will. There are many Indians yet. We come three hundred at this time. You must consider the Indians lose nothing but their life. You must lose your fair houses and your cattle.

The note perplexed the soldiers and finally they gave it to the Massachusetts government which decided it had been written by an Indian called James the Printer who, in the days of peace, had helped the Apostle Eliot print the Indian Bible.

16. THE DEATH OF
CANONCHET

All that winter the Indians stayed hidden in the western wilderness. Although the warriors emerged to raid settlements and farms, they disappeared as quickly as they had come. The white troops that pursued them never caught them.

Next morning the troops might stumble on the traces of an Indian camp: the smoldering embers of a fire, the marks left in the snow by wigwams, the scars made in the earth where the Indians had dug for ground nuts, the skeleton of a horse's head or hoof that showed that a handful of the Indians had feasted well the night before. But the Indians themselves had vanished; they had packed up their wigwams and moved on.

Not only were the Indian warriors living like fugitives in the wilderness, their squaws and children, their old people and the sick and wounded were with them. Sometimes, in a village pitched in the snowy woods as

lightly as a bird perching for a moment on a tree, lived
all that remained of a once-proud tribe.

With them, too, were their English prisoners and
from such of these as lived to tell the tale have come
curious glimpses of the tribes in flight. Homeless,
hungry, and desperate as they were, the Indians clung
gallantly to their love of colorful costumes and fine
ceremonies.

One of the prisoners, Mrs. Rowlandson, later wrote
a book about her captivity among the Indians and in this
book is the following description of a dance in which
Queen Wetamoo, who was Philip's sister-in-law, and
her Narragansett husband, Quinnapin, participated:

Quinnapin was dressed in his Holland shirt, with great laces sewed at the tail of it; he had his silver buttons, his white stockings, his garters were hung round with shillings and he had girdles of wampum upon his head and shoulders.

Wetamoo had a kersey coat, and covered with girdles of wampum from the loins upward. Her arms from her elbows to her hands were covered with bracelets. There were handfuls of necklaces about her neck, and several sorts of jewels in her ears. She had fine red stockings, and white shoes, her hair powdered and face painted red that was always before black. And all the dancers were after the same manner.

There were two others singing and knocking on a kettle for their music. They kept hopping up and down one after another, with a kettle of water in their midst, standing upon some warm embers to drink of when they were dry. They held on till it was almost night, throwing out wampum to the standers by.

Toward the end of the winter the Indians congregated at Squakeag (near Northfield) on the banks of the Connecticut River. Here they would fish for salmon in the spring run. Here they would plant their seed corn when it was fetched from the secret pits in the Narragansett country.

In the second week in March King Philip arrived at Squakeag. He had been gone all winter, trying to get help from the Mohawks near Albany.

"What do the Mohawks say?" asked Philip's allied

chiefs around the council fire that night. "Will they join us?"

"No," said Philip. "The Mohawks have not seen what we have seen. They have not learned that the white man is the enemy of all Indians."

The chiefs were disheartened by the news.

"How can we go on fighting by ourselves?" they asked. "Our warriors are hungry. All winter we have had but little to eat."

"We shall fish in the river," answered Philip. "We shall plant our corn."

"Our seed corn is in the Narragansett country," grumbled the chiefs.

"Has no one been to get it?" asked Philip angrily. "Are we Indians unable to provide for our people as the white man provides for his?"

There was silence. Raising the corn was work for the squaws and not for the braves.

Then Canonchet, the Narragansett chief, spoke up, "I will go back to my country. I will bring the seed corn from the corn pits, and I will fight along the way. What warriors will go with me?"

"I will go with you," said a young brave.

"And I will go," said another.

"And I."

Chief Canonchet picked thirty volunteers. They set forth together and on March 16, at the Pawtucket River, ambushed an English captain named Pierce, with

his company of fifty Plymouth soldiers and a score of friendly Indians, and killed nearly everyone. Then the Narragansetts split into small bands and raided wherever they could.

On March 27, some of them descended on Providence, Rhode Island, where their old friend, Roger Williams, lived. Williams was now a captain in the Providence militia, but wishing to make a final effort to keep peace, he went forth alone to meet the Narragansett braves, with just a cudgel in his hand.

"Massachusetts can raise thousands of men to march against you," he warned the braves. "As fast as the men of Massachusetts fall, the King of England will supply other men to take their places."

"Well, let them come," answered the braves. "But as for you, Brother Williams, you are a good man. You have been kind to us for many years. Not a hair on your head shall be touched."

True to their word, the Indians did not harm Roger Williams, nor did they harm any of his family. But they burned his house along with fifty-three other houses in the settlement. Several colonists were killed.

The burning of Providence was the last of the Narragansett victories. Soon fresh troops were scouring the country for the Narragansett braves and above all for Canonchet.

In the first week in April the troops searched along the Pawtucket River, where Canonchet had ambushed Captain Pierce. Two old squaws told the troops that Canonchet was staying in a camp nearby. The squaws pointed the way, and some of the soldiers and a few Pequots who were fighting with the troops crept up to his camp where he sat in his wigwam. He was wearing the silver-laced coat the colonists had given him the year before to persuade him from joining King Philip. Around his shoulders he had thrown a scarlet blanket, and he was entertaining several of his braves with an account of Pierce's defeat.

When Canonchet looked up and saw the soldiers, he leaped to his feet and fled from the wigwam, still wearing his scarlet blanket. Not until he reached the open was he able to cast aside the blanket. As he ran along the river, he cast aside the coat. He ran swiftly, but a Pequot gained on him and forced him into the river. While Canonchet was crossing the river, his foot slipped on a stone, and his rifle, going under water for an instant, was rendered useless. He made no resistance when the Pequot seized him.

A young soldier went up to Canonchet and, in a spirit of admiration, asked him a question about his battles.

"You are a child," said Canonchet. "You do not understand matters of war. Let your brother or your chief come. Him I will answer."

The captains offered Canonchet his life if he would command the Narragansetts to surrender.

"I know the Indians will not yield," he answered.

The captains told him he must die.

"I like it well," he said. "I shall die before my heart is soft or I have said anything unworthy of myself."

They led Canonchet onto the plain at Stonington and ordered him to be shot by three Indians who were fighting on the colonial side. The captains believed it would demoralize the hostile Indians to know that Canonchet, the greatest Indian warrior in New England, had been shot by men of his own race.

The guns were fired, and the bronze body of the Narragansett chief slumped to the earth. The soldiers cut off his head and sent it as a trophy to Hartford, Connecticut.

17. THE TRIBES DESERT KING PHILIP

The death of Canonchet disheartened the Indians, as the colonists had predicted. He had been King Philip's strongest ally, and his valor and fame had helped keep the tribes together in the face of disaster. Although they had killed many Englishmen and cattle and burned innumerable houses and barns, they themselves had lost their hunting grounds and gone hungry for more than a winter.

Let Philip coax them now with all his mighty eloquence. He could never rekindle their vision of an Indian union. They were too hungry and discouraged, and after Canonchet was killed, they fell away from Philip. One by one, or in little bands, or by tribes, they deserted him. Those who remained loyal to him continued to raid English settlements throughout the Colonies. Bridgewater, Chelmsford, Weymouth, Sudbury . . . it would take too long to name them all.

And with each attack the colonists' terror of Philip increased. By now they really considered him a fiend and a ravenous beast.

Occasionally a stray report cast a softer, kindlier light on his reputation. Mrs. Rowlandson, the white captive who had been ransomed in the spring, told her English friends how she had met King Philip several times while she was with the Indians. On one occasion Philip had asked her to make a shirt for his little son who was staying with some neutral Indians in the Narragansett country. Philip paid her a shilling for the shirt.

On another occasion she was journeying with the tribes to Mount Wachusett, where her ransom money would be paid.

"A bitter, weary day of it I had," she told her friends afterward. "I had been traveling now three days together, without resting any day between. At last, after many weary steps, I saw Wachusett hill, but it was many miles away.

"Then we came to a great swamp through which we traveled up to the knees in mud and water. It was heavy going to one already tired. My strength was almost spent, and I thought I would sink down at last and never get up. But I may say, as in Psalm 94.18 'When my foot slipped, thy mercy, O Lord, held me up.'

"As I went along, having my life, but little spirit, Philip, who was in the company, came up and took me by the hand and said, 'Two weeks more and you shall be Mistress again.' "

Certainly those two incidents proved that Philip had a kindly streak in his nature. But the fiendish image the colonists had formed of him remained unchanged, and the terror inspired by his name grew daily.

In May, the Indians who were still loyal to Philip gathered at the fishing grounds at Peskeompskut (now called Turner's Falls) on the Connecticut River, between Northfield and Deerfield. One evening, Captain Turner, who had marched from Hatfield with one hundred and eighty men, surprised a camp of these Indians as they lay in their wigwams. Many of the braves were killed before they could reach the open. Others were shot down as they fled in their canoes and still others, who had hidden among the rocks, were seized and slaughtered. Afterward the soldiers burned the wigwams and destroyed the Indians' supplies of fish and ammunition, as well as two forges for mending rifles.

The noise of the battle had reached two other Indian camps, one across the river and another on an island about a mile downstream. Warriors from both camps appeared suddenly and in their turn surprised the English, who were drunk with victory. Captain Turner had difficulty in bringing his men together, and to add to the confusion a young trooper called out, "King Philip is coming! King Philip is coming with a thousand Indians!"

The sound of King Philip's name produced a panic among the troops, and as the Indians surged forward,

the panic turned into a rout. Although King Philip did
not appear, the troops fled on. Captain Turner was
killed, and Captain Hadley, taking over the command,
managed to bring the men to a semblance of order. But
the Indians pursued them through the woods and the
dark ruins of the town of Deerfield and almost to the
doors of Hatfield.

Although the latter part of the battle was an Indian
victory, the first half had been a disaster from which
the tribes did not recover. It dashed their hopes of lay-
ing up a store of fish and other food, and it destroyed
their chance for sallying forth to keep the settlers from
returning to the ruined villages in the Connecticut

valley. One by one the settlers reappeared, replanted their fields, and began to rebuild their homes.

In early July, the Wampanoags, the Narragansetts, the Pocassets, and the Sakonnets drifted back to their old haunts in the east, and the colonists were powerless to cope with the bands of desperate Indians who laid waste to the countryside.

18. BENJAMIN CHURCH
JOINS THE HUNT

Benjamin Church, the settler from Sakonnet, the Black Goose country, had claimed all along that the colonists did not know how to fight the Indians. Church had served twice with the Plymouth troops: once in the Mount Hope campaign and later in the invasion of the Narragansett country. After each campaign he had retired in disgust at the high command. He was a quarrelsome, cocksure fellow, and his superiors were not sorry to see him depart; but they knew his worth as an Indian fighter.

In April, 1676, when it seemed likely that King Philip and his Indians would soon return east, the Plymouth council of war had sent for Benjamin Church, told him they planned to dispatch a company of sixty or seventy soldiers to the outlying towns of the Colony, and asked his advice.

"Sixty or seventy men!" snorted Church. "But first

122

let me say that if I take command of men, I shall not lie in any town or garrison with them. I shall lie in the woods, as the Indians do.

"Now, as for numbers, the Indians will probably return in great quantities. For us to send out only small companies of men is to deliver them into the enemy's hands.

"Gentlemen, send no less than three hundred soldiers. I myself will recruit one hundred and fifty colonists if you will add fifty more, as well as one hundred friendly Indians. With such an army I can do good service. I shall accept no other terms."

The councilmen shook their heads.

"We are already in debt," they complained. "We could never pay for such a big army, and we will not employ Indians. Your advice, Mr. Church, is impractical."

Church returned in a huff to his temporary home on the island of Rhode Island. Then one day, while cutting a small stick, he cut his finger too, and looking upon this as an omen, he resolved to go to war again.

On June 8, he reappeared before the Plymouth councilmen. Although the island of Rhode Island lay next door to Plymouth Colony, travel by land was almost impossible because of the enemy, and Church had been obliged to sail by sloop around Cape Cod to Plymouth. The councilmen greeted him cordially and told him they were glad to see him alive.

"And I am glad to see you gentlemen alive," retorted

Church. "I've seen so much fire and smoke on your side of the country that I feared you had all been destroyed. Gentlemen, what are your plans for fighting this war?"

"Providence has brought you here at the right moment, Mr. Church," replied the spokesman for the council. "This very day we decided to send out an army of two hundred men, two thirds of them English and one third Indian. This, to some extent, resembles the plan you formerly proposed to us."

The news put Church in a good humor, and he agreed to return to the island of Rhode Island to see what men he could muster among the refugees who had fled there after the destruction of their houses in Plymouth Colony.

On his homeward journey, Church passed near Sakonnet Point and saw some Indians fishing on the rocks. He himself was in a canoe, because something had happened to his boat and he had been obliged to get two friendly Indians to paddle him the rest of the way. As the canoe glided closer to the rocks, he recognized the fishermen as Sakonnets and members, therefore, of the tribe he knew so well. The tribe, ruled over by his old friend and neighbor, Queen Awashonks, had been fighting on Philip's side, though at the outbreak of the war Church had almost persuaded the queen to remain neutral.

He now called out to the Sakonnets on the rocks and at the risk of his life went ashore and spoke to them, for he felt that if he could see Awashonks he could induce her to desert Philip.

"Where is Queen Awashonks?" he asked the fishermen.

"She is in a swamp three miles away," they answered. "She has left Philip and does not intend to return to him. You wait here, Mr. Church. We will bring her to you."

"No," said Church, thinking it wise to speak first to the government officials on the island of Rhode Island and try to get their sanction for such an important undertaking, "not today. But I will come back in two days and meet Queen Awashonks and her son, Peter, and her chief captain and the warrior, Nompash, at the rock at the end of Captain Richmond's farm."

When Church arrived on Rhode Island, he told his tale to the government officials. They declared he was mad to think of returning to Awashonks, for he would surely be killed. If he did go, it would be without their permission.

Church went, taking with him a bottle of rum, a roll of tobacco, an English friend, and the two Sakonnets who owned the canoe. He found Awashonks, Peter, Nompash, and the chief captain at the appointed rock, and the queen shook his hand, saying she was glad to see him. Then they all moved back into the grass where they could talk more at their ease.

Suddenly, out of the tall grasses, burst a horde of

painted Indians with guns, clubs, spears, and hatchets.
There was a moment of dead silence. Then Church said
to Awashonks, "Your Indian told me two days ago that
you wished to see me and discuss peace with the
English."

"That is true," replied Awashonks.

"Well," said Church, "when meeting to treat of
peace, it is customary to lay aside one's arms."

"What arms shall we lay down?" asked the queen.

Church caught the grim look on the warriors' faces.
"Oh," he said lightly, "your men need lay down only
their guns—just for form's sake."

Every warrior put down his gun and then joined Church and Awashonks. Church pulled out his bottle of rum, poured some into a shell and asked the queen, "Did you live so long at Mount Wachusett as to forget to drink 'occapeches'?"

He drank to the queen's health and passed the shell to her. She seemed suspicious and bade him drink again.

"There is no poison in this rum," he said, and took a good long drink, which reassured the queen. She drank too, and passed the shell among her attendants. When the last drop had disappeared, Church distributed the tobacco he had brought, and the words began to flow freely.

Awashonks said to Church, "Why didn't you come to Sakonnet before this? You promised me you would come last year. If you had come, I would never have joined Philip against the English."

"I couldn't come because the war broke out so suddenly," explained Church. "But early in the war I went as far as Punkatees to see you. I was attacked by a great many Indians and fought all afternoon, though I had only nineteen men and was not prepared to fight."

At the mention of Punkatees, the warriors had risen and begun to shout. A big, sullen Indian raised his tomahawk and would have killed Church if some of the others had not intervened.

The interpreter turned to Church and asked, "Do you know what that big fellow said?"

"No," replied Church.

"He said you killed his brother at Punkatees," explained the interpreter. "He thirsts for your blood."

"Tell him his brother started the affair," said Church. "If he had stayed at Sakonnet as I wished, he would not have been killed."

The chief captain of the Sakonnets interrupted. "Silence," he said. "Speak no more about old things."

Everyone sat down again and discussed peace with the colonists. Awashonks finally agreed that if Plymouth would promise to spare the lives of all her tribe and to send no one out of the country, the Sakonnets would subject themselves to Plymouth and serve Plymouth to the best of their ability. Church said he believed the Plymouth government would agree to this request.

The chief captain rose to his feet and bowing to Church, said, "Sir, if you will please to accept me and my men and will lead us, we will fight for you and will help you to King Philip's head before the Indian corn is ripe."

Before the Indian corn was ripe! That was the kind of talk Church liked to hear, and he hastened to send word to Plymouth that Queen Awashonks and all her tribe would desert King Philip and join the English if her conditions were accepted.

Plymouth finally agreed and after considerable deliberation instructed Awashonks to take her tribe to Sandwich, on the coast of Cape Cod. She was to travel by land and Church by way of the sea, for the woods

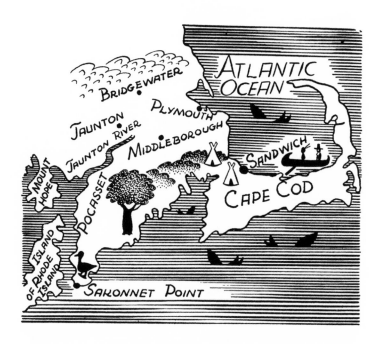

bristled with hostile Indians only too ready to kill a white man.

Church and three companions reached Sandwich late in the afternoon of July 23 and looking down at the shore from a distance, they saw the Sakonnets working and playing by the sea. All the tribe—men, women, and children—were there. Some were galloping along the sand on horses; some were playing football; some were racing; others were digging for clams; and still others were out fishing on the sparkling waters.

When Church joined the throng, he was led to a shelter that had an open side facing the sand and the sea. Queen Awashonks and her councilors came there to welcome him, and the tribe shouted with delight. Then the Indians scattered and returned ladened with the tops of dry pine trees which they piled in a great heap on the sand.

After the sun had dropped behind the sea, the Indians lit the pine tops and the whole tribe gathered in rings around the giant blaze. In the first ring, next to the fire, knelt the queen and all her oldest men and women. In the second ring stood the lusty warriors, and behind them gathered the rest of the tribe.

Then the chief captain stepped up to the fire with a spear in one hand and a hatchet in the other. As he danced around the fire, he named each tribe and sub-tribe hostile to the English. Whenever he mentioned a name, he drew out a firebrand and fought it. And when he had listed and fought all the enemies, he stuck his spear and hatchet in the sand and stepped back to make room for the next Indian who repeated the ritual. The chief captain explained to Church that they were making soldiers for him.

After all the braves had participated in the ceremony, Queen Awashonks and her chiefs moved over to Church. "Now we are engaged to fight for the English," they said. "Call for us at any time, all or any of us, as you wish, to fight the enemy." And they presented him with a handsome rifle.

Church thanked them for the rifle and their kind offer to help. Then he selected a few of their warriors and next morning set forth with them to Plymouth village.

They reached it the same day. On the following day, July 24, Governor Winslow, who was pleased with Church's success with the Sakonnets, gave him some English soldiers to add to his Indians.

Better still, the governor handed Church the following commission:

"Captain Benjamin Church, you are hereby nominated, ordered, commissioned and empowered to raise a company of volunteers of about two hundred men, English and Indians . . . you are to take the command, conduct, and to lead them forth now and hereafter, at such time, and unto such places within this Colony, or elsewhere within the Confederated Colonies, as you shall think fit . . ."

Command as he saw fit! That was enough for Church. He did not stop to raise more soldiers, but set forth that night with those he already had. They marched fifteen miles through the woods and before daybreak reached Middleborough, an old haunt of the Indians.

Church fully intended to capture King Philip, dead or alive, before the corn was ripe.

19. BEFORE THE CORN
WAS RIPE

King Philip had returned to his boyhood haunts around Mount Hope. Sometimes he was reported to be along the shores of the bay, and sometimes inland among the woods of pine he loved so well. A warrior who had deserted him told the colonists, "Philip has come home to die like a chief, with his arms folded across his breast."

Most of the deserters still admired their chief, but they lacked his will and the singleness of his purpose. They felt an overpowering doom descending on them, against which they could no longer struggle. As warriors, defending their tribe, their families, and their hunting grounds, they had never been afraid to die. But now that their tribe had been destroyed, their hunting grounds taken, and their families sold out of the country into slavery, it was hard for them to remain valorous to the end, like Philip. Weakly, in a daze, they drifted over to the strong side of the English.

The faithful few who stuck to Philip cared nothing

for the risks they took in wreaking destruction wherever they could, and the symbol of their destructive power was King Philip. To the colonists, he was the savage beast who had laid waste to New England, killed five hundred of their people and ten thousand of their cattle, raided forty towns and burned one thousand barns and houses. No Englishman could rest until the arch-rebel had been captured and killed.

So they hunted him down like a fox. Connecticut and Massachusetts soldiers joined in the hunt but Captain Church, with his band of Plymouth men and Indians, was the best of the hunters. His methods were unique, for he made each band of Indians he captured lead him closer and closer to King Philip's lair.

Church captured Indians with amazing speed and success. He began capturing them as soon as he reached Middleborough on July 25. There, in the swampy thickets, he took a band of Wampanoags and Narragansetts by surprise and made captives of them all. Then he questioned them and made them tell where he could find more Indians, and off he marched and seized another band. And so it went. And out of his Indian captives he made good soldiers.

He would say to them, after they were taken, "See here, my fellows, I like you, and if you will be my soldiers, you shall not be sold out of your country."

If an Indian looked wild and surly and began to mutter, Church would clap him on the back and say, "Come, come, you look sullen now, but that means nothing. My best Indian soldiers were like that when they were taken. After you have been with me for a day, you will love me, too, and be as brisk as any of them."

Many of the captured Indians did grow fond of Church, and served him briskly.

At the end of July, Captain Church learned that King Philip was heading toward the great Pocasset swamp which had sheltered him so well the year before. Church arranged for extra troops from Bridgewater to join him at the edge of the swamp.

On July 30, while the Bridgewater troops were marching to the rendezvous, they discovered a band of Wampanoags and Narragansetts at the Taunton River. The braves had felled a huge tree and were using it as a bridge for crossing the stream.

The troops fired, and during the skirmish that followed, a soldier shot at an Indian who looked like King Philip. The bullet hit its mark and as the Indian toppled, another warrior at his side escaped into the bushes. The soldier saw, too late, that the man who escaped was King Philip, disguised to resemble his uncle, and when the Indians withdrew into the swamp, the troops discovered that the uncle was the man who had been killed. Another of Philip's family was a victim of the skirmish. This was his sister, who fell into the enemy's hands.

Next day Captain Church and his men marched in pursuit of King Philip. When they reached the tree that spanned the river, they saw an Indian warrior sitting motionless on the tree stump, as if lost in thought.

The Indian's face was turned and Church, believing him to be an enemy, raised his gun.

"Stop!" said one of Church's Indians. "Don't shoot. That is one of our own men."

The Indian on the stump turned quickly. It was King Philip!

Church's Indian fired, but like a flash, before the bullet was over the stream, King Philip had leaped from the stump and vanished.

Church and his troops crossed the river as fast as they could, and next day stole up to Philip's headquarters in the swamp. So unexpected was their arrival that King Philip left all his wampum behind him when he fled. Among the Indians taken prisoner were King Philip's wife and little son whom he adored.

An Indian who had deserted to the English said to Church, "You have now made Philip ready to die, for you have made him as poor and miserable as he used to make the English. You have now killed or captured all his relations. Soon you will have his head. This bout has almost broken his heart."

Rapidly, as the cornstalks grew higher under the warm August sun, the last of the Indian rebels were being rounded up.

On August 11, Queen Wetamoo, sister-in-law of King Philip and squaw sachem of the Pocassets, was discovered by the English in a swamp near Taunton. They captured some of her people, but she herself escaped and tried to cross the Taunton River on a raft. The river is wide at its mouth and she did not reach the opposite shore alive. Nobody knows what happened. The English, however, recognized her body when the tide washed it ashore and they cut off her head and sent it to Taunton.

On the day Wetamoo died, Captain Church was marching toward King Philip's old home, the hillock of Mount Hope. Church had, for a guide, a Pocasset Indian named Alderman, who had come to him recently and said, "My brother told Philip to make peace with the English. And for those words, Philip killed my brother. Now I shall have my revenge. I shall lead you to Philip's camp."

Shortly before dawn, on August 12, Church, Alderman, and a band of Indian and English soldiers drew close to Philip's camp in a swamp at the foot of Mount Hope. Church gave an officer a few men and told him to steal up to the camp at daybreak, surprise the Indians while they slept, and drive them from cover. "Have your men shout when they chase the Indians," Church instructed the officer. "We shall shoot anyone who isn't shouting."

Church stationed an Englishman and an Indian in pairs behind each important tree around the swamp.

Dawn broke, and the rifles cracked in the camp. Then the bushes stirred and King Philip appeared. He had fled so quickly that he had had time only to pull on his underbreeches and stockings and to seize his gun. Alderman and his English partner were nearest to Philip. The Englishman aimed and missed fire. But Alderman sent a bullet into Philip's heart.

King Philip fell on his face in the mud of the swamp, with his gun under him.

20. THE LEGEND

Captain Church ordered his men to cut off King Philip's head and quarter the body. The four parts of the body, except for the famous hand that had been twisted when an English pistol split in it, were hung on four trees near the swamp where King Philip had fallen. The hand was given to the Indian who had shot him, and the rascal pickled it in rum and earned money by exhibiting it in the Colonies.

King Philip's head was sent as a trophy to Plymouth village, where it remained on a spike outside of the fort for twenty-four years. Then at the dawn of the new century, in the very year of 1700, New England's most eminent divine, the Reverend Cotton Mather, visited Plymouth village. When he walked by the fort and saw the whitened skull, he reached up his hand, removed King Philip's jaw, and spoke contemptuously of the defeated chief.

A few years later the Reverend Mr. Mather, in his history "Magnalia," described the incident so that future generations might share his hatred for King Philip and the vanished Indians. "The hand which now writes took off the jaw from that blasphemous Leviathan," declared the Reverend Mr. Mather, "and the renowned Samuel Lee hath since been pastor to an English congregation, sounding and showing the praises of Heaven upon that very spot of ground where Philip and his Indians were lately worshipping the Devil."

The words of the Reverend Mr. Mather always stirred his audience profoundly. But the words and the ideas of Roger Williams, which were spurned during his own lifetime, may outlive those of the Reverend Mr. Mather. There is still hope that somewhere in the world the various people, regardless of customs and color, can live side by side, in peace. It is a pity that the white men crushed their Indian brothers in New England.

After the war, King Philip's wife and young son were sold into slavery in the West Indies. Thousands of Indian captives were sent into slavery or killed. Some of the uncaptured Indians fled north into Canada or westward, beyond the Connecticut River. A few who had been neutral or friendly during the war were permitted to remain in New England. But the strength of the Indian people, who had been as much a part of New England as the trees and the rocks, was destroyed.

For a while the colonists were glad to forget King Philip's war which had brought sorrow or death to every English family in New England. It was a relief to have the question of the ownership of New England settled

NEW ENGLAND

KING PHILIP'S
CAMP

CONNECTICUT RIVER

KING PHILIP'S
STOCKADE

KING PHILIP'S
HEADQUARTERS

KING PHILIP'S
SPRING

KING PHILIP'S
CAVE

KING PHILIP'S
OAK

KING PHILIP'S
CHAIR

KING PHILIP'S
EATING ROCK

for good. The English farmers, as they plowed and seeded the land inherited from the vanquished enemy, took satisfaction in realizing that they would give the soil better care than the Indian hunters had ever given it.

But try as they would, the colonists have not been able to forget King Philip. His ghost haunts the hills and the forests, not only in the east where he lived, but throughout New England, wherever his Indian rebels fought the white men.

To quiet the ghost, the colonists have named many landmarks in honor of King Philip. Numerous are the caves, each one called King Philip's Cave, where he is supposed to have hidden when the colonists were hunting for him. Numerous are the mountain lookouts from which he watched the burning of an English village, and the springs where he and his warriors quenched their thirst after a bloody raid. And there are several flat-topped, sprawling rocks where King Philip, according to legend, picnicked frequently with his wife and little son in the happier days before the war.

The legend of King Philip, the man, is changing, and the devilish image of him, which was so deeply engraved on the colonists' minds by the conflict, is beginning to fade. In its place emerges the truer image of a noble Indian who fought bravely against the doom descending on his people, and in spite of the injustice dealt to him and all his race, kept in his heart a natural grace that was part of the untouched forests and the pure, fresh wildness of earliest New England.

PRONOUNCING
DICTIONARY
OF INDIAN NAMES

The colonists in New England frequently spelled and pronounced an Indian word in several different ways. Some of the Indian names in this dictionary have entered our English language, and the spelling and pronunciation which usage has stamped on them are given below. For the unfamiliar names, we can do no more than indicate pronunciations that seem reasonable in the light of the little that is known today about the Indian language in King Philip's time.

Algonkin (ăl-gŏn′ kĭn). The group name of all the Indian tribes inhabiting New England.

Awashonks (ä-wä′ shŏnks). The queen, or squaw sachem, of the Sakonnet Indians.

Canonchet (kăn-ŏn′ chĕt). The Narragansett chief who was

King Philip's greatest ally. Canonchet was the son of Miantonomo and the grandnephew of Canonicus.

Canonicus (kăn-ŏn′ ĭ-kŭs). The Narragansett chief who befriended Roger Williams and gave him the land where Providence was founded.

Cheeshateaumuck (chē-shă-tē-ä′ mŭk). The only Indian who graduated from Harvard College.

Connecticut (kŏ-nĕt′ ĭ-kŭt). A word meaning "long river" or "river of pines." The Connecticut River, flowing from north to south through the length of New England, marked the western frontier of the Colonies. The Colony of Connecticut borrowed her name from the river.

Massachusetts (măs-ă-chū′ sĕts). The name of the tribe that lived near the present site of Boston. The Colony of Massachusetts borrowed her name from the tribe. The word is a combination of *massu* (great), *adchu* (hill or mountain) and *set* (in the region of).

Massasoit (măs′ ä-soit). The Wampanoag chief who befriended the Plymouth colonists and was the father of Alexander and Philip. The word, Massasoit, is believed to mean "he who is great" or "the leader."

Metacom (mĕ-tä′ cŏm).   ⎱ Two of King Philip's Indian
Metacomet (mĕ-tä′ cŏm-ĕt). ⎰ names.

Mohawk (mō′ hôk). The name of a tribe living west of the Connecticut River, in the present State of New York.

Narragansett (năr-ă-găn′ sĕt). The name of the tribe living on or near the western shores of Narragansett Bay. The word is believed to mean "people of the small point."

Nipmuck (nĭp′ mŭk). The group name of various Indian tribes living near the Connecticut River and its branches.

The word means "fresh water" or "in the region of the fresh water."

Nompash (nŏm' păsh). One of the Sakonnet warriors.

Nunnuit (nŭn' wĭt). One of Queen Wetamoo's husbands. His real name was Petownonwit, but the colonists found it easier to call him Peter Nunnuit.

Pawtucket (pô-tŭk' ĕt). A river flowing into Narragansett Bay.

Pequot (pē' kwŏt). The name of a once powerful tribe in Connecticut Colony. The Pequots rose up against the colonists in 1637 and were crushed.

Peskeompskut (pĕs-kē-ŏmp' skŭt). An Indian fishing haunt, now called Turner's Falls, located on the Connecticut River, between Northfield and Deerfield.

Pocasset (pō-că' sĕt). The name of a tribe living on the eastern shores of Narragansett Bay. The queen of the tribe was King Philip's sister-in-law, Wetamoo.

Pokanoket (pō-kă-nō' kĕt). The name of an old confederacy of tribes in the Mount Hope region. The Wampanoags were the leaders of the confederacy, but by King Philip's time the ties of union had become extremely weak.

Pometacom (pō-mĕ-tä' cŏm). One of King Philip's Indian names.

Punkatees (pŭn-kä' tēs). A point of land on the eastern coast of Narragansett Bay, in the Pocasset country. It is also called Pocasset Neck.

Quabaug (qwô' bôg). The name of one of the Nipmuck tribes. The Quabaugs inhabited the region around Brookfield.

Quinnapin (quĭ-nä' pĭn). The Narragansett warrior who was Queen Wetamoo's last husband.

Sakonnet (să-kŏn′ ĕt). The name of a tribe living on or near the site now occupied by the town of Little Compton, R. I. The word means "haunt of the black goose."

Samkama (săm-kä′ mä). A signer of the treaty King Philip made with Plymouth in the fall of 1671.

Sassamon (săs-ä′ mŏn). The Wampanoag Indian who betrayed King Philip.

Squakeag (sqwô-kē′ ăg). An Indian fishing haunt on the Connecticut River, near Northfield, where the Squakeag Indians used to live.

Uncompaen (ŭn-cŏm′ pēn). A signer of the treaty King Philip made with Plymouth in the fall of 1671.

Wachusett (wä-chū′ sĕt). A mountain in Massachusetts, about thirty-five miles east of the Connecticut River. It was a Nipmuck stronghold.

Wampanoag (wŏm-pä-nō′ ăg). The name of King Philip's tribe. Some experts have said that the word means "custodian of the imperial shell"; others, that it means "eastern land."

Wamsutta (wŏm-soō′ tä). The Indian name of King Alexander.

Wequomps (wē′ quŏmps). A mountain in Massachusetts, near the Connecticut River. It is now called Sugarloaf Mountain.

Wetamoo (wē-tä′ moō). The queen, or squaw sachem of the Pocasset Indians. Her husbands included King Alexander, Peter Nunnuit and Quinnapin.

Wispoke (wĭ-spō′ kē). A signer of the Taunton treaty of April, 1671.

Wocokon (wō-cō′ kŏn). A signer of the treaty Philip made with Plymouth in the fall of 1671.